ACKNOWLEDGMENT

Child of Zimbabwe tells the tale ~
my life, from birth through to exile ~   ... ~
a narrative of traumatic experience, an ~ asy
trawl through painful memories that seeks to
challenge, inform and inspire. It is my one
opportunity to speak out on behalf of all of the
young people all over the world who have
experienced similar situations to me; those who
have been victims of child abuse, of slavery and
neglect, of beatings, torture and rape; most
crucially, of a lack of love.

In recording these memories and re-opening
unhealed wounds, my main aim is to provide a
reminder of how important it is that we love and
live our lives without harming each other. However
terrible my experiences have been, it is only
through living this life that I have learnt how to
grow, and how to summon the courage to conquer
despair and raise up my head to the sky.

In writing this book, I have grappled with the ideas
of forgiving and forgetting. In a life like mine, one
is left with two choices: to forgive and move on, or
succumb to the anger and hate. I am not seeking
revenge; to forgive takes far more courage than
that. Yet forgetting is even less easy; my identity
lies in these memories; they are my scars of
bravery and determination, my shining stars of

hope. It has taken a great deal of soul-searching to unravel my past and discover my purpose on earth.

Throughout this book, I have deliberately chosen not to talk of my love for God often. I leave it up to each reader to decide who it was that helped me survive this ordeal; who offered me hope and comfort and love; and who allowed me in time to arrive at a clear understanding of my own inner beauty.

Each one of us is part of a wonderful creation. I have suffered; I have cried; I have learnt. With God's grace, I look forward to a brighter future.

This is my story.

CHILD OF ZIMBABWE

BY DEBRA MINA CHIDAKWA

Published 2008 by arima publishing

www.arimapublishing.com

ISBN ... 549 287 8

© Debra ... kwa 2008

Edited by ... el Cherry

Cover design by ... an Alexander

All rights reserved

Printed and bound in the United Kingdom

Typeset in Arial 14/16

Swirl is an imprint of arima publishing.

arima publishing
ASK House, Northgate Avenue
Bury St Edmunds, Suffolk IP32 6BB
t: (+44) 01284 700321

www.arimapublishing.com

CHAPTER 1

I sometimes wonder how I came to have so many names. All I know is this: each name arrived with a story. Chenzira was the very first. Chenzira: "by the side of the road".

On the day I was born, my mother boarded a bus called Shu–Shine. With my father, she was heading to the city of Gweru, where women would travel from all over the Midlands Province for the birth of their children. Aside from the one at Pakame Mission and the one near Boterekwa Mountain in Shurugwi, Gweru had the only maternity hospital in the whole of the province. It was the biggest, and by far the most popular. The Mission maternity hospital was only visited by those who were very poor, or those who wished to cook food on their own, away from their wicked mothers–in–law, who, they suspected, would make a meal of their babies, starting with the placenta, immediately after the births. By the side of a red asbestos building, heavily pregnant women would set up camp, waiting two, maybe three weeks for their new-borns to join. During the day, they would tire themselves out in the Mission's small vegetable garden, though they were never allowed to harvest the big green tomatoes or delicious chomolia that grew; these would be uprooted by others, and either sold back to the women themselves or taken to Cha-Cha-Cha market to be sold at a small stall beside Chakamanga butchers.

The other maternity unit at Shurugwi was only meant for the miners' wives; it had limited space and could never have coped with all the thousands of women in the province. Besides, many women chose Gweru because they were scared of being marched up and down the twisted Boterekwa Mountain. Expectant mothers were expected to exercise; at both Pakame Mission and Shurugwi hospital, there was always that terrible mountain to climb. Women would often be seen gathering in prayer, making desperate pleas for their babies to arrive early, before the senior midwives could call for the dreaded "big exercise", which involved all the women who had just started labour pains, as well as all those who were well overdue. At Pakame Mission, the matron, with a whip or wooden spoon in hand, would lead the pregnant women to Guru-guru, the highest hill-top in Pakame, before chasing them back down its slippery slope. When the women reached the camp, they were sure to have their babies soon. Some wouldn't even make it all the way back; their babies, tired of bouncing, would simply pop out at the foot of the hill. Many children were given the name Chimukungurutse, which literally means "one who came rolling down the hilltop like dung".

At Pakame, you would often see women being carried in wheel-burrows back to the camp as they screamed with the effort and pain of their final pushes. The matron, ever watchful, commanded a group of charmless nurses who hovered nearby with razor-blades, threads and salted water. The razor-blades were there to cut the umbilical cord, and the salted water was to wash hands and sterilise thread, which would be tightened around the stump of the cord like a noose. As well as these implements, the matron would hold a flat cooking stick for slapping the fleshy bottoms of expectant mothers whenever she deemed them not to be pushing sufficiently hard, or opening their legs sufficiently wide. If the baby's head was thought too big, the razor would be used to extend the opening. The matron would then sew up the tear with a thread like a fishing line. Clever women tried to escape this fate by preparing the baby's opening with German laundry soap or ruredzo herbs, which took on the slippery nature of okra when soaked in water. This herb, which grows almost like a climbing flower, can spread for miles and miles and is found all over the great valleys of Zimbabwe.

Guru–guru was known to be a holy hill. It was rumoured that great ancestor spirits dwelt there, and the fact that no trees grew was widely held as a sign of impressive age. Bald and round like an old man's head, the hill stood out for miles; a huge, immovable space-craft. On rainy days and early mornings, Guru-guru would become slippery, and local youths would climb its sides with bottled delight, sliding back down on the bark of the munadzwa tree. This tree, according to my grandmother, was also a good omen for pregnant women. If you were ever to find a python that had swallowed a calf or some other animal and was now sated, at the point of falling asleep, you should take a nice, long stick from the munadzwa tree, slowly massage the python with it, then force the stick right in its mouth, inducing a powerful vomit for use on any woman experiencing delayed or complicated labour. With the stick still wet, draw a line down from the top of the woman's head; as soon as you reach her legs, the baby will surely pop out!

In times of drought, Guru-guru hill was used to appease the ancestor spirits and call on them to summon the rain. This was called Mutoro. Mediums and bone-throwers would gather on the hill and dance for a whole seven days. They drank African "seven days beer" and ate un-salted, roasted meat; some, depending on rank, would even devour the blood of freshly slaughtered animals. Invariably, as soon as the seven days were done, the sound of thunder would boom through the province and the whole sky would darken with pregnant clouds of rain. The eldest women would halulate and cheer the thunder's roar, while youngsters would jump up and down in the villages, praising the ancestors for hearing their prayers. When everyone had reached the bottom of the hill, a wondrous downpour of sweet rain would begin, lasting at least seven days, or long enough for the people to plough their land.

Things these days are different. The white-man brought in his magic of impregnating the clouds with powder; with it came more and more drought in my country. I can't help but believe that something upstairs was seriously disturbed. It must also be said that, nowadays, many people don't believe in the traditional healers and spirits; in God, we have found a higher medium than our own ancestors. People still respect the ancient traditions – they are a part of us, they make us who we are – but they no longer worship the traditional spirits with such infinite trust and concern.

On the Shu-Shine bus, my parents were travelling from Nhema region, from a village known as Ziyambi. Our Head Chief was Nhema and, when he died, his name lived on, though his successor was really Dayidayi. Nhema Tribal Trust Land, as it was officially called, is a part of the larger town of Shurugwi. Of course, the white-man labelled these areas differently; it may have been difficult for them to pronounce the guttural Shona words, or perhaps this was simply a sign of the disrespect shown to black people during the colonial era. To the white-man, my country was always Rhodesia, named after Cecil John Rhodes, who now lies buried in Bulawayo, our second city, nestling in the Matopo Hills. In 1980, the Chimurenga war liberated the black people of Zimbabwe. That is a long story, and I will make no attempt to narrate it here.

On the journey to Gweru, my mother fell into the final stages of labour. The driver pulled over in the middle of the jungle so that my father could improvise a "clinic" by cutting down branches from the mutundo and musasa trees, softening them with leaves from a fig tree to make bedding for his wife and their new arrival. These trees are a vital resource in my country. The musasa tree has good timber and, during the summer, people used to pick delicious caterpillars from its bark. Those that survived would transform into some of the most beautiful butterflies in our country, if not in the whole of the world, though I never thought too much about that, for fear of losing my appetite - those caterpillars, with hot chillies and a glass of sweet wine... oh my!

The mutundo tree has beautiful leaves that provide excellent shelter during the summer season. Its bark is also a good remedy for stomach pain, and is widely used to make whips for herdsmen to control their cattle or establish their territory. When I was a child, those whips had a powerful language all of their own; lashes could be used to warn of imminent danger, offer plentiful honey to share, or suggest it was time to head back home and put the cattle to bed in the kraals. Sadhiba Terri, our dip-tank supervisor, was renowned for his ability to play a very romantic tune on his whip. This talent gained him a beautiful wife in the village, and I believe many other women wanted to bed him, even many of those who were married. Needless to say, he was a very envied man, and rumours inevitably spread that some of the local children belonged to Terri, even when there was already a man in their house!

Enough of this spiteful gossip! The whips were more practically used to warn of the arrival of MuBhunu, the big bearded white farmer who owned most of the land in our area. Herdsmen would chase their cattle off of the green grass of the white man's farm, driving them back to the local valley, where the grass was limp and dry. Many herdsmen were too scared to take their cattle out onto the white man's farm at all; if caught, they faced arrest or fines of twenty-five shillings a cow, with confiscation the unavoidable result of unpaid dues. As a result, some of the cows grew so thin you could count the ribs protruding from their hide; push one with your hand and it would fall to the ground like a child. Many cattle died on their own, of malnutrition, before even facing the slaughter. In such cases, no-one liked to eat the meat, which tasted of rubber and bubbled extravagantly as it cooked on the fire.

Most of the land in my province belonged to MuBhunu; us black people were left to divide up dry and unfertile acres, which were often very rocky and sandy. The fence of MuBhunu's farm almost touched our village, so that even childish exploration often descended to the level of trespass. Good rivers with plenty of fish flowed through that farm, and there were sweet wild fruits and wild game animals and plentiful fire-wood. Women used to make dangerous treks into the farm's deep forest, risking capture in the pursuit of dried wood for their fires. What they feared most was being caught by MuBhunu's black workers, who came from the same village as the women but were merciless in their beatings; some would even rape the women, all in the name of a few stolen sticks!

Apart from my father, everyone feared MuBhunu almost to the extent of worshipping him as a god. This made my father very angry; he would call his fellow villagers cockroaches because their cowardice led them to sneak into the village kitchens, searching for food and scattering guiltily as soon as the owners appeared.

The Shu-Shine bus carried on for the city, leaving my mother and father with no choice but to deal with the situation alone. There was no alternative for the driver, who had to continue with the journey in order to meet the timetable stipulated by his road permit. As well as over a hundred and twenty passengers, there were also a good number of chickens and goats, all on their way to Makaranga market for sale. The name Makaranga simply means "black person of a Shona speaking dialect". During the colonial era, it was used to degrade us black Africans; it came to mean "nigger market" or "kaffir market". In the true sense, though, Makaranga is the name of a tribe of Shona-speaking people, who come mainly from Masvingo Province. Many tribes are spread across my country's regions: the Mandebeles from the province of Matabeleland, the Makarangas from Masvingo, the Mazezurus from Mashonal, and the Manyikas from, unsurprisingly, Manyikaland. These are simply a few; our strong regional identity feeds rivalries and prejudice to the point that it is even difficult to marry someone from another province; most such marriages still end in divorce, and sometimes even in murder.

My province, the Midlands, now has a mix of all sorts of people from all different regions; even foreigners from Zambia, Malawi or Mozambique are now settled there. There are also rumours that some of our most prominent government figures come from Zaire and Tanzania, and these rumours may well be true; after independence there were many suspicious occasions when we were only told about the origins of a minister's mother or father, and not of both of their parents. Some of their family names were never heard of until their owners had come to power, which has led many to believe that, despite our struggle, we are still being ruled by foreigners, making a mockery of those who died in the fight.

At the time of my birth, or so my father said, a group of baboons had gathered on a small hill-top to watch in keen anticipation. Doves cooed sweetly to announce my arrival, and a large python was woken from its slumber by the enticing smell of blood. As I entered the world with a piercing shriek, the baboons chuckled and jumped up and down, and the father baboon made a booming sound that shook the whole forest, causing the doves to scatter out of the trees and the python to slink stealthily towards my parents, already busy burying the placenta. The snake got bigger and bigger, aroused by the screams of a baby craving the first drop of its mother's milk. My father said it was as though my cries had woken the whole of the jungle. The cucaboro, the forest's alarm, was singing its song of forewarning, and my parents didn't hang round to see what would happen; with quickened footsteps, they took me off into the jungle.

After a long day plodding through the thick forest, we arrived at a farm where we were fortunately able to stay with one of the workers, a gardener and butler called Mr Chibonga. My mother was very weak and tired - she had lost a lot of energy - and Mrs Chibonga, who later became my godmother, hurriedly offered her porridge, water to drink and a hot salted bath. Mrs Chibonga was also known as Mai Kaimoni; as far as I'm aware, this name was derived from their white boss, who used to bully his workers by constantly shouting "come on!". When she gave birth to her first child, a boy, Mrs Chibonga named him Kaimoni.

Years later, when I came to know the Chibongas again, they had left the farm and moved to a village very close to ours. Their youngest son, Biggie, was very naughty; he would often walk up and down the valley, hunting bullfrogs with a bow and arrow. Of this behaviour, Mr Chibonga was strangely proud; he rarely missed an opportunity to paint Biggie as a heroic warrior to anyone who'd listen.

It was my father who was really a hero. I don't remember seeing him at all before the age of six; soon after my birth, he was taken to a detention centre called Hwahwa, then on to Gonakudzingwa, where all prominent political activists were held. My father was so deeply involved in the struggle for our country; he lived and breathed politics all through his life, right up to its bitter, bloody end. His was a family of warriors and hunters; his great grand father, Ulha'nganyani ("Who have you met?"), fought the Boers at the battle of Lalapansi, leading warriors, armed with bows and arrows, spears and stones, against white settlers, armed with rifles. At one point, he shouted "lalapansi amadhodha!", ordering his warriors to lie down and play dead after failing to fend off the bullets with their shields made of animal hide. Despite their disadvantage, my great-grandfather and his warriors still managed to bring down quite a few of the Boers; a lot of blood was shed that day, and the site of the battle is still known to this day as Lalapansi. In fact, it is not very far from where I was born; I am very proud to have begun my life near a place where my ancestors walked.

During his hunting days, my father would bring home a lot of game meat and wild sweet honey – often enough to feed the whole village. He had twelve hunting dogs, of which Waintanga and Major were the ones I liked the best due to their size and beauty. Jambo was the biggest; he had large lips and ears and was roughly the size of a young calf. His bark was as frightening as thunder. My father would set traps in the fields to keep the baboons from stealing our maize. One day a big baboon with a blazing red bottom was caught; he was probably the father baboon, and was struggling to free himself from the trap when my father appeared on the scene. My father threw his spear but missed, so he approached the baboon with his knob-kerrie to strike. This proved a mistake; the baboon somehow caught both the weapon and my father; there was a struggle, my father was down, the baboon on top, smacking him and rolling him round in the dust. With fists that would stay swollen for weeks, my father struck the animal with blow upon blow, eventually pounding the side of its head with one final thrust, and leaving him dead in the dirt.

Word of my father's bravery spread like a forest fire through the village and beyond. The man who became a hero for killing a baboon was soon to become one for his contribution to the armed struggle in my country.

By the time I started school, my name had changed to Mina'ngedwa: "I Alone". Mrs Chibonga, however, had nicknamed me Chipida because of my well-rounded bottom, which made me so very good at dancing to the drums, particularly *chips, agogo* and *whishu*. I was one of the prettiest girls in school, or so I thought; my mother used to dress me in mini-skirts or flowery dresses, which came from the Dorothea Group, a West German organisation that helped the families of those in political detention. Christian Care, a charitable organisation in Gweru, had referred my mother to the group and some of the other members used to come to our village on visits. They were exciting times for our family when those kind and generous people travelled all the way from West Germany to my mother's humble home. It was also interesting, if somewhat confusing, to see a group of white people assisting a black family who were trying to overthrow the white people from our own country. I had no idea that there were different types of white people, with different languages and different ways of living.

How I used to love those European clothes! When I had the chance, I would stare at myself, over and over, until my neck started to hurt. Unfortunately, there were no mirrors in my mother's home; most of the time it was left to other people to comment on how well dressed you looked, or whether the clothes fitted or not. Jealous people would rarely tell the truth, so the best mirrors were often found on the surfaces of still ponds; the colours were blurred and distorted, but you got a decent idea of how pretty you looked. Unfortunately, this was hardly a harmless pastime; much fear was involved in searching still waters for self-approval. It was said that such vanity could upset a mermaid, one of the dark spirits of the underworld. The danger was considered particularly acute for those who were light skinned, or those who wore red clothes!

That wasn't all I had to fear. As a young girl, I always dreaded arriving late to school. Mr Nemapare, the headmaster, would wait for all late-arrivals with a long stick, freshly snapped from the branch of one of the school's many gum-trees. His whippings were very painful indeed; the whole rest of the day, your legs would be covered with painful, visible marks, which sometimes developed into sores. This was the norm; no parent was supposed to complain, and those who tried were seen as ridiculous or branded as varoyi - "witches". Often, I would wet myself even before my turn came up; the headmaster would either leave me alone in shame or, turning a blind eye, would continue to deal out my painful share of the beatings. The urine made every stroke sting even worse, as if salt was being rubbed into my open wounds!

Despite, or perhaps because of, my fear, I was always one of the brightest pupils at school. When I was only in grade 3, I had an essay read out at assembly, in front of the whole school. It was called "The Day I Will Never Forget", and it got twenty out of twenty and became the talk of the whole village. The intense jealousy of other pupils and parents caused my mother to fear for my life; she was frightened that witches would send their tikoloshis - little men from the graves - to beat me up! Being pretty and intelligent definitely had its downsides; senior pupils bullied me badly, but worst was the private abuse I often received from the teachers themselves. My class-teacher took to pinching me under my skirt, between my buttocks and thighs; while he shouted at the other pupils, I would feel his sweaty, crusty hand on my leg and see his other hand move in his pocket. I felt so embarrassed, dirty and useless; I knew that something was wrong but didn't really understand the meaning of these routine individual punishments.

One day, I finally found the courage to tell my mother after she had seen the horrible pinch marks while helping me to take a bath. My explanation horrified her, and she went straight to the school headmaster. Unfortunately, he'd already heard - and believed - rumours that my class-teacher's wife was a powerful witch, and was consequently reluctant to take any action. In the end, it was me who ended up facing the painful punishment of cleaning the whole schoolyard and digging a rubbish pit; if I didn't complete the task within five days, my headmaster would add in a hundred strokes for fun. To this day, I don't understand why I was punished for telling the truth; perhaps this is partly the reason that I now study law. When a new headmaster arrived, my faint hopes that times would change were quickly doused when he humiliated me on his very first day. Speaking at assembly, he reminded all of the pupils that if they were to go home and report any of the activities from school without telling the headmaster first, they would be severely punished, just like Mina - me.

I remember the first time I saw myself in a real mirror. One of my teachers sent me to his house to fetch ballpoint pens; when I opened the door to his bedroom, I was amazed to see a young girl in a blue floral dress, just like the one I was wearing! I stood still; the girl did exactly the same. My heart was pounding with fear. I was convinced I was watching a chitikoloshi – one of the little men, the poltergeists, who walk by night. I slammed the door, ran back to class and went straight to the teacher, trembling.

"Sir, I think you should come with me. There is a girl in your bedroom!"

"What girl?", my teacher asked.

"Please sir - just come." I had started to cry. Instead of taking me back on my own, my teacher asked all of the class to join us; now even the big boys and girls who had been sniggering fell silent. The walk was like a funeral march; no-one said a word, and I'm sure I saw one of the big boys making the sign of the cross. In the bright morning sunshine, fear was engraved on our faces.

When my teacher opened the door to his bedroom, there was a loud cry of amazement.

Once calmed, each of us took turns to look at ourselves in the mirror. This proved a turning point for all concerned, not least one little boy, Lloyd, who finally saw what the rest of us had been seeing for years: a line of thick green bogey hanging out of his nose. It used to peep out, and he would drag it back in by breathing so heavily and disgustingly that you would swear you were in the presence of a pig! Sometimes, he would do it in break-time when you were just about to tuck into a snack from home; I often gave most of my food away due to Lloyd's disgusting behaviour. After the day with the mirror, there was a definite improvement in cleanliness among us all.

One day, during school break, the head teacher called my brothers, my sister and I to his office. At first, I feared we were all set to be expelled; my mother had been one of the last to pay the building fund and school fees. We looked at each other before entering the office, but nothing was said; none of us had any idea what lay in store. To our surprise, the head teacher seemed happy to see us; he was smiling from ear to ear as he told us not to worry, but to go back to class, pick up our books and head immediately home, where our mother was waiting. He said nothing more, but was obviously pleased by the secret he hid.

On the way home, we debated and asked each other endless questions. My brother was convinced that someone was dead; perhaps grandmother, or one of our aunties or cousins, or maybe something terrible had happened to our father at the detention centre, or even to our mother herself? No! Not mother, please God! The last time we had visited our father at the detention centre, he had been planning with friends to dig a tunnel and escape to Mozambique, or Lorenzo Marques, as it was known at the time. They planned to take the midnight train, which passed every night just a few miles away from the centre. Could he really have escaped?

There was so much fear and excitement as we headed home. Mother was waiting for us by the front gate; she was smiling and told us to follow her up to the big peach tree, where a man with a very long beard was resting in an arm-chair, wearing a big leather hat that almost entirely covered his face. On hearing our footsteps, the man lifted his head and revealed himself as our father. He smiled and stretched out his hands to greet us; we rushed towards him and almost toppled him over. There was laughter and tears of joy; even the birds and bees that surrounded us seemed to be celebrating. Father told us there was no longer a Gonakudzingwa, but that on public holidays and at other times the police would come to pick him up and take him to the nearest remand or detention centre, which was either Shurugwi, Gweru or a notorious local prison named Wha-Wha after the way tortured men would wail in pain like dogs. Prisoners at Wha-Wha would sleep naked on wet floors, enduring electric shocks until they finally submitted and denounced the revolutionary parties. Some were castrated with pliers; others died of all kinds of "accidents" or "illnesses"; many took their own lives. We knew that the reasons given were not the accurate causes of death. We knew that many died in the hands of their tormentors.

People from all over the province travelled to greet my father, who seized the opportunity to teach the value of independent thought and introduce others to ZAPU, the revolutionary party. He claimed that the struggle was continuing, and that more was on its way. He told of revolutionary friends who had escaped to Mozambique and Zambia to prepare for the civil war. He warned us to expect bloodshed; it was the only method left, he said, of showing the white men that us blacks meant business and could claim back our country, Zimbabwe. It was the only way, he said, to show them who's boss.

In the evenings, father would make us sit round the kitchen fire, singing revolutionary songs late into at night. Sometimes, when the moon was weak, he would wake us up in the middle of the night and lead us out to MuBhunu's farm to burn a tobacco field or cover the cattle's dip-tank with stones. We were like mini guerrillas; arriving home, covered in mud and bruises, we would feel ferociously proud, but exhausted, and frustrated by our inability to tell anyone in the village. Despite our silence, the police didn't hesitate to arrest my father on many occasions. They snatched him away for days on end; he would always return, bruised, battered, but desperate to continue the fight for what he saw as the greatest prize of all – freedom!

One Easter holiday, the police came to arrest my father as usual. He had done something terribly bad and, with it being a public holiday, the police didn't want him spreading his black politics. My father saw their truck at a distance; he was thatching my mother's hut. By the time he'd climbed down the wooden ladder, the police had already reached our gate, forcing him to flee with no shirt on or shoes, nothing but his khaki shorts. The white policemen chased after my father, ordering him to stop, but he just carried on towards the fields, now green with tall fresh maize crops, many of which were destroyed by the ducking and diving. At one point, the police nearly caught him; they threw their handcuffs, trying to catch him on the legs, but missed and he managed to escape. How could they catch him, a hunter who was used to chasing wild animals? The handcuffs got buried in the fresh ground; we watched on as the policemen tried in vain to find them. The police left with neither handcuffs nor prisoner. As they climbed into the truck, they loudly offered a reward of twenty five dollars for anyone who found and returned the handcuffs. They also called out a warning: if my father didn't hand himself over within twenty-four hours, they would come back to arrest my mother instead. If they found him, he'd be in prison for life.

Later that day, when he came out of hiding, my mother begged my father to hand himself in. He finally agreed to go the next day; he was given a thorough beating and spent the whole week naked, trapped in a cold cell, with water up to his ankles. This treatment would make people shiver continuously and end up pissing themselves, hallucinating or even worse. The water would stink like sewage and, each morning, the prisoners would be doused in it as a wake-up call, causing many of them to catch terrible diseases like pneumonia and tuberculosis. There was no point even asking for a blanket; it would simply be thrown on the floor. Those prisoners lucky enough to be put in dry cells had to endure blood-sucking lice, which added an extra creepy layer to their blankets. None of the guards took any notice of the conditions, the diseases or the mental distress. The prisoners were black kaffirs; who was to care?

One early morning while my father was in prison, my mother found the handcuffs in the field and brought them home, placing them carefully on the table in the dining room. She had a visitor that morning, so she asked my brother and I to go and play outside. We decided to go to the dining room and take a closer look at the cuffs; they were just lying on the table so my brother suggested we play a game of police and thief chase. I was the thief and my brother was the policeman, chasing me round the table, shouting for me to stop. When I did, I held up my arms in surrender and allowed my brother to click the handcuffs round my wrists; game over.

Unfortunately, when I went to take off the cuffs, I found that I couldn't. We pulled as hard as we could, but, if anything, it only made them tighter. I was now in pain and started to cry; I called for my mother, who quickly came to see what all the fuss was about. She brought in her visitor, the head-teacher's wife, and together they tried soaping my hands in foamy water. Nothing worked. In the end, my mother had to take me to MuBhunu's farm to ask if he could unlock the handcuffs, or perhaps call the police on his phone. We walked for about four miles; whenever I needed some water, mother would have to pour it into my mouth and, whenever I needed to use the toilet, she would always have to help me, telling me off as she did. The big white man took a good look at me and laughed so hard I thought he might fall over. He told my mother that he didn't have any keys to unlock the handcuffs, and that, furthermore, it was illegal to tamper with government property. ! He agreed to call the police instead.

We waited at the farm, in a barn that stank of cow dung, until the police truck arrived very late at night. They hadn't brought any keys for the handcuffs, so they took us back to town in their truck; as I sat in the back, I noticed that the policemen wore sandy khaki uniforms with the silver letters B.S.P, standing for British Special Police. They had long grey socks, which almost touched their knees, and well-polished brown leather shoes. Around their tunic coats they wore a well-polished brown leather belt, in which they kept a whistle, a wooden baton and handcuffs and sometimes a small handgun. Their outfit was completed by a cap that matched the uniform and almost covered their faces. The ride to Shurugwi police station was a very bumpy one; my mother looked increasingly worried as she stared at my swollen hands.

The handcuffs were removed, with some difficulty, as soon as we got to the station. I was given the twenty-five dollars reward, and my mother and I slept in one of the empty cells; we were even given clean blankets to use for the night. We got home the next day to find the whole village telling our story. My brother had even been given a new nickname: Sergeant Major. The head teacher's wife told the story at the next school assembly. Not for the first, or last, time, I was to become the local joke.

My mother gave birth to ten children: five boys and five girls. Most of the pregnancies were conceived during trips to my father's detention centre. My mother was also an active and well-respected figure in the fight for independence. She was tireless, and her education played an important part in her life. When my father was given a few days at home, he would always return to a beautiful house, with cows, chickens and a very big orchard, full of all different kinds of fruits. This was my mother's work, and he must have been pleased to have such a wonderful wife and a great mother for his children. He was grateful for what she had done, but there was also resentment towards her; she had taken most of his responsibilities and left him feeling very insecure among his own family.

His attitude began to change dramatically. He was no longer the loving father, the revolutionary, the hero; he became a fearsome man, who never smiled in front of his family. He barked orders, making us work very hard; his punishments became more and more severe. Sometimes, he would even beat my mother. He became so controlling, so unloving, that we all came to fear him; in fact, the whole of the province came to fear him. Mother would ask God to change her husband's heart, just as he had done with Saul on the road to Damascus. Whenever there was lightning in the sky, I would think it was God attempting to strike down my father, trying to transform him, to return him to his previous state. Closing my eyes, I would see Saul persecuting all the good people, cheering at the stoning of Stephen, and then being struck by that all-powerful bolt. I, too, used to pray for such a life-changing experience to occur to my father. It didn't work; he treated us more and more like dogs and began to beat my mother so badly that it caused the whole family to fall apart. It was so sad for my mother to see the man she loved abusing her and beating her children for no real reason. I did everything my father ordered, everything I could to stave off his beatings. My brothers and sister were different; they would challenge him, ending in serious beatings that made me feel guilty and sore, as if I was the one who'd been punished. I knew I was a coward, but my brothers and sisters thought I was favoured; father rarely beat me, though mother did at times, like when I forgot to wash the pans, or when I broke her umbrella, thinking I could use it as a parachute to jump from the big blueberry tree. I also broke my ankle, but that didn't stop mother from beating me hard, even as I tried to explain I was just copying Mr Baboon and Mr Monkey, who had used an umbrella to fly from tree to tree in a story we'd heard on the radio at school. My mother loved her umbrella so much; owning one was a very prestigious thing in our village.

My brothers and sisters grew increasingly distant, making me yearn for the beatings that would make me more like them, more acceptable to my own family. Yet I was also a coward, trying to save my own skin. In the end, it seems I paid the price for this cowardice; I was unforgivable, no matter how hard I tried to reach out and form a meaningful relationship with my siblings. Maybe it was just my guilty mind, which failed to recognise their pain and see their love for me. I know deep down in our hearts, we did, and still do, love each other very much.

My father, meanwhile, was becoming an increasingly Pharaoh-like figure; we were the Israelites in bondage, and life was growing unbearable. The whole village knew what was happening; my father was not only terrible to us, he also bullied all of the men in the area. Everyone became fearful, recognising the anger and awful resentment that had built up during those weeks of torture in the detention centres. Something terrible had gone wrong with my father. My brothers took horrible beatings, but it was my sister who became his main punch-bag. Despite his behaviour, we continued to love and respect him. Mother told us to keep on praying, but father hated to hear Jesus' name in the family home; he used to say that it was the white man's propaganda, which they'd used to help colonise Africa. He said that the white man left bibles in our hands as they stole all our diamonds and gold. He warned that if he ever caught us kneeling and praying to Jesus, our lives would end there and there. So we used to say our prayers during his absence, with someone standing outside to keep watch. If the alarm was raised, we would stop immediately and start rushing around, pretending to be doing our chores. Only mother refused to stop; this was seen as a big challenge towards father, and was definitely one of the main causes of arguments and beatings.

On Sundays, my father would always go out of his way to find work for us all, just to stop us from going to church. I never complained or made excuses; I just carried on with my chores, even when I was feeling ill or exhausted. My two older brothers left home at a young age to look for work. This was the start of my family's slow separation; we began to communicate less and less, as confusion, misunderstanding and animosity took control. Time is a great healer, and I hope that one day we will all come together and heal the wounds of our painful memories.

At one point, my mother couldn't take any more; she packed her bags and set off for her parents' home near the southern mining town of

Zvishavane. As father took out his frustrations on my sister, life became so bitter and painful that people in the village advised us to run away and follow our mother. One day, when father had gone out hunting, we decided to do just that. We packed nearly everything, including our mother's live chickens. We cooked some supper for father, left it by the fire place as usual, then walked miles to catch the midnight bus to the south. We had no money for the fare, so my sister had to explain the whole story to the driver. Fortunately, he came from the Shiri clan, just like our mother; we took our seats and slept the whole night through.

The next morning, we collected our luggage and set off towards my mother's family home, about four miles walk from the centre of Zvishavane. Halfway there, we bumped into mother and her two sisters, who were on their way to town to go shopping and sell some hand-made table clothes and crotchets. They were so shocked to see us; mother was shaking because she knew that father would soon follow and that there would definitely be big trouble to pay. Indeed, after a few weeks at the house of my grandmother, who was very kind and happy to see us, father found us and took the opportunity to bring mother home, too. He was crying, and brought gifts of three lovely dresses for mother and sweets and biscuits for us.

Mother finally agreed to come home; it was obvious that she still loved him and wanted to give him a second chance. She was convinced that this time he was really going to change, and, for a few months, at least, she seemed to be right. But father just couldn't forgive my sister for leading us off; eventually, he gave her the beating of her life, practically killing her. After that, she became very quiet, and isolated herself from her friends. Watching my sister, who had once been such a happy young girl, completely broke my heart and made feel so useless that, once more, I wished it was I who had suffered. If only I wasn't such a terrible coward!

My mother used to tell us of the time she met my father. He was a handsome man, almost six feet tall, with warrior's shoulders and a lion's broad chest. What struck her at first was his nose; it was straight and long, like the Tower of Lebanon, overlooking Damascus. My father didn't have the kind of African nose that is as wide as rhinoceros' - the type of nose that a bullfrog could jump into easily, along with his mistress. He had the nose of a missionary, almost a Mediterranean nose. At the time that they met, my father was working at a hotel near the Great Zimbabwe Ruins in Masvingo (then Fort Victoria) as a hotel chef and entertainer. My mother's older sister was married to a man who worked at the same hotel; she introduced my future parents, and it was while my father was playing his guitar and calling out his name -

Ishmael Muneri Chuma - to a rapturous audience that my mother fell in love. She knew right away that this man would be her husband. In spite of all the pain he caused her, my mother never lost that love. I could never understand how she could love someone who continually disrespected and abused her. Perhaps it was a love born of fear.

During the struggle to liberate Zimbabwe, my mother was battered and bruised, arrested several times and her home became the main hospital for wounded "freedom fighters". When no-one else was interested in liberation, my mother would walk miles and miles, staging small rallies and meetings and teaching people the value of being in an independent country. It was hard work; our province was also home to the then prime-minister, Mr Ian Douglas Smith. People used to be given a cup full of sugar if they showed their support for Smith on Rhodes Founders' Day and at Easter and Christmas. Naturally, my family never received any goodies; in fact, we were branded as "terrorists", and some people in our village used to say we were a public nuisance and threaten to burn us in a hut full of petrol. My mother was never frightened at all. I am convinced she got this courage from the visits she made to my father at the detention centre in Gonakudzingwa. My mother campaigned strongly against the detention laws, especially when prisoners were kept naked during cold winter days.

I was already fully aware of, if a little confused by, everything that was going on. By now, my elder brothers and sister were often taking part in the mini rallies staged by my mother. At night, we would sit by the fire in our hut and sing all the songs of struggle. Mother would end up praying for all of the political prisoners and their families, including my father. If she had known that the fight would bring nothing but grief to her family, perhaps she would never have bothered. Perhaps she might. All I am sure of is this: my mother was a bird that was never meant to be caged. She fought the good fight, and was left deeply hurt by all the unfairness in the aftermath of the struggle, all of the lies and greed that was later to be shown by most of our so-called leaders. Someday, someone will find the courage to re-write the history of how we became liberated in Zimbabwe.

My mother now fights a different struggle; she has devoted her life to God's work. In spite all of her sorrow - her husband is dead, in some unknown grave, and she rarely enjoys the fruits of independence - she has become a village health worker, a Methodist preacher and a wonderful grandmother. Through everything, she has kept her head high. When she goes up to heaven, her head will be high. She will have a good place; she deserves it.

CHAPTER 2

At the age of nine, I was sent out to work.

One day, I came home from school and found mother talking with one of the men of the village. My father had been hunting for three days now, and mother and the man were sitting under the big mango tree, each holding a big juicy mango. My mouth watered; I started to look for my own, the biggest one in the whole of the tree.

My mother was startled.

"Mina!", she called. "What kind of behaviour are you trying to show to our visitor? Have you forgotten your manners, you silly child?"

By the tone of her voice, I could tell that I'd caused some embarrassment, and that, if I failed to respond appropriately, I would definitely pay for it later.

"Good afternoon, Uncle Shoko", I said, in a very polite and sorrowful voice.

"Good evening, Mina." He winked and continued munching his mango. Most of his mouth was covered in juice; it ran all the way down his beard. He looked completely disgusting. My mother gave a stern look; Mr Shoko's visit was apparently more serious than I'd thought. In fact, it was me he had come for. At first, I felt very important; Mr Shoko wasn't anyone to admire, but the fact that he was much older than me, and that he had taken pains to travel in such hot weather to see me, was enough to swell my pride. Little did I realise that his visit would change my life forever. In not so many words, I was informed that it was expected of me to go to the town of Gatooma - now Kadoma - and work as a childminder/housekeeper for one of Mr. Shoko's immediate relatives. The name of this lady was Mama Kuda, and she was a teacher at Zhombe Mission. Her husband worked at the Bata Shoe Company factory in Gweru.

Of this situation, my father was fully aware; he had simply left mother to do the dirty work. I had so many unanswered questions. Why did I - the middle child - have to be picked, from all of the other children? Was it to punish me for trying too hard, for being too obedient, for avoiding the beatings? Why should I become the bread winner when there so many other alternatives; my two eldest brothers, for instance, could have helped if the situation had really become all that bad. Why me? This bitterness was mixed with a little excitement; after all, I was off to the city, to live with the rich and mighty, eating bread and butter everyday. I started to daydream, mumbling the little English I knew, in case "madam" only understood that language. By being in the city, I thought, my hair would naturally become straight and long, suiting my complexion and making everyone jealous when I returned to my village. I would look like an English lady of mixed race, and my small nose, which had often been likened to a rabbit's, would grow long and straight, with a beautiful bridge like the white ladies had. Everyone would stare at me, struggling to speak because I would only be talking in English. Oh yes; no more sadza for me, only rice and chicken, with fresh salad, and ice-cream for desert. I had no idea how English food tasted, and had never even licked an ice-lolly; all I knew about city food had come from one of the local villagers who was a kitchen boy at a white man's farm. He used to talk of the breakfasts he cooked for his boss; eggs "sunny-side up", with sausages, mushrooms and fresh tomatoes, all washed down with a glass of juice. Then, at ten o'clock each day, he would make tea in a bone-white china pot, and serve it with fresh scones and a delicious slice of water–melon.

Oh yes! In the city, I would be rich. I could see myself now, driving a red sports car down Boterekwa, along past Cha-Cha, Chirashavana, Hanke Mission, Dombwe, and on into my village. I would come home with sweet toffees for my brothers and sisters; with tins of biscuits, loaves of bread; with sun jam, buttercup margarine, self-raising flour for mother to make "fat cooks"; dripping for frying green cabbage; all sorts of other items for the family grocery. I would find a night school, continue my education; that was very important to me. At this point, I would drift into a deep sleep, awaking only to re-plan my future life in the city. Or, sometimes, if I had forgotten to empty my bladder, awaking to a slap on the face from my sister and a long night to be spent soaked in urine.

I only had two days to prepare for the journey. It would be my first time to travel alone, and I felt entirely unsure of the future. Despite all my fanciful daydreams, I was very upset at the idea of having no choice. Holding back tears, I began to pack up all of the toys that I used to play with under the big mango tree: empty tins of jam; dolls made of maguri; a variety of rags and twigs that I pretended to use as cooking utensils. My mother told me to throw them away; I did it with a broken heart. I didn't even have the chance to say bye to my local school friends; mother didn't want anyone to know what was happening and told me not say anything to anyone, not even my teachers. My sister let the cat out of the bag by telling one of Mr Chibonga's daughters, who kept making fun of the story, laughing about it and telling nearly everyone in the village, if not beyond. I brushed off her laughs; she was only jealous that I was going to the city to start paid work despite being many years younger than her.

Mother seemed very sad; I couldn't understand why she would let me go if it wasn't making her happy. Later on, I learnt that mother had played only a very small part in the arrangement; it was father, of all people, had done the deal. The idea was to ease the financial burden on my family, and all of my older brothers and sisters were to be sent off in similar ways at a later stage. My older sister was sent to live with our aunt - our father's sister - who owned a farm in Mashaba. Later on, my aunt's husband - an old man, with many missing teeth - was meant to take my sister as his second wife. The man was a drunkard; he beat my aunt so nearly to death that she ended up walking sideways like a crab. He may have been a good farmer, but that didn't give him the right to even think of accepting my sister.

"If that lizard", she once said, "even so much as touches me, I'll fry his balls for breakfast." She later told me that she used to sleep with a small pocket knife ready to chop off his balls. Of course, I knew she was never capable of doing such a horrible thing; she was simply expressing her anger. I couldn't help feeling that, although my father was very politically active, his visions of family values were completely messed up. He was dividing us, cutting us off from all that we'd ever known. Leaving mother was one the most cruel and difficult experiences that ever happened to me, but, as the black sheep of the family, I came to grow used to this punishment. In fact, I even came to feel like a stranger within my own family; I was so confused and isolated; was I really that different from others?

In the end, all of us were sent to live with other families in different parts of the country. Our communications, our relationships, broke down. Sometimes, it remains hard to understand each another; my siblings have all grown so different, though we still love each other in our own unusual ways. There is so much pain and sadness, so many unanswered questions, but also so much hope for a brighter future.

When the morning arrived, I woke up early to catch the six o'clock bus to Gweru. It was still dark outside; the cocks were crowing, but peace was in the air. I felt that excitement again; I was off to live in the city. On the bus, a few people were already waiting, including Mr Shoko, who had reserved me a place right beside him. The driver blew his horn for the last time, and a few stragglers ran onto the bus, thanking their ancestors for helping them reach it on time. I could smell their unwashed armpits, and the sweet smell of sleep on their bodies. One lady who sat in front of us had a pair of knickers protruding from her chest; she must have shoved them in her bra, but her huge breasts were forcing them out. Most of these people were obviously planning to wash in the toilets near Makaranga market before proceeding with their businesses. All they had to do was carry some

Vaseline on a piece of paper, along with a little broken mirror and an Afro comb for the difficult knots in their hair. For a toothbrush, they would use a small stick from the muchekesani tree, which was well-known as a good remedy for sore gums and toothache. In fact, it also worked as an antibiotic and mouthwash.

The conductor was still on top of the roof, arranging all of our luggage; he remained there even after the bus had begun to move, so that we could clearly hear him whistling and banging, practically dancing with excitement. This was pretty normal; bus conductors were natural show-offs, who liked to stay for a while on the roof of the bus, before swinging down like Tarzan and sliding through the half-open door with exquisite confidence. This was a very dangerous thing to do, of course, and some conductors were even killed by their stupid stunts.

On the bus, there were dogs, chickens, goats and all sorts of small parcels lying all over the place and making it extremely difficult to put your feet down without stepping on something. When we got moving at speed, the conductor started whistling with excitement, encouraging passengers to sing and tap their feet on the zinc floor tiles. Dust flew up everywhere, and the whole bus swayed from side to side, at times avoiding the sharp boulders protruding across the narrow road; at others, the lazy donkeys that refused to clear the way. I wondered how the driver ever managed to see his way through all the confusion, and I finally realised why he had to drive atop a huge cushioned pillow; otherwise, he would have constantly cracked his backside against the countless humps and bumps of the road. I suddenly felt a pang of isolation; I was missing my family, felt frightened, and tears were in my eyes. Nobody noticed, or, if they did, they must have thought it was due to the cold morning air, which was making a lot of eyes watery.

By the time we reached Cha-cha-cha, the bus was fully packed. People ran past the windows, offering all sorts of cooked and uncooked food for sale. My stomach rumbled; I'm sure Mr Shoko heard the noise because he dug in his big brown overcoat and produced some home-made bread - chimed - that still bore the fingerprints of his wife, as well as a few burnt patches and a strangely unappetising smell. Mr Shoko's overcoat was so greasy - it had probably never been anywhere near water, other than rain and dew. Yet it was a somewhat famous coat; it had been part of the dowry paid when his first daughter, Majasi, got married. Looking at the crumbled dirty bread, I suddenly lost my appetite, which seemed to please Mr Shoko, who pushed so much of the bread in his mouth that, for a second, I could have sworn he was about to choke. His eyes bulged and he made a strange loud noise through his throat, attracting a lot of attention. Leaning out the window, he hurriedly bought some fizzy drink - a Fanta Orange, I think - from one the vendors. Trying desperately to open it with his teeth, he only managed to cut his gums in the process, causing blood to dribble from the corners of his mouth. Blood mixed with home-made bread was a terrible sight that I hope never to have to witness again! Yet worse was to come: Mr Shoko started to hiccup badly. He downed his drink, attempting to stave off the burps, but Fanta fizzed through his nose; some even fell back in its bottle, with pieces of homemade bread for new company. Still Mr Shoko belched; in fact, he belched so loudly that it sounded like someone had just blown a trumpet. He took two more huge sips, then turned towards me and offered the bottle. I politely refused.

When things settled down, I drowned in the smell of diesel and woke up to find that the bus had arrived at Makaranga market in Gweru. We were in the city! Mr Shoko carried my small bag as he guided me to the next stop, where we got on a local bus to Mkoba Township. This bus was very different from the one that had brought us from the village; the people here were very clean, aside from a few who I took to be beggars or tramps, or perhaps workers returning from industrial sites. I felt excited again, and wanted to get a good taste of this city society, where everyone looked happy and rich. I started daydreaming of all the good things I would do as a city girl. I promised myself that I would work very hard, so that my boss would be happy to help me to finish my studies. That was still very important to me.

The house, when we arrived, looked very much like all of the other houses in Mkoba; they were all built in the same style, and so closely resembled each other that it was really quite tough to tell them apart. The only way to know which one was yours was to remember the door number and the name of the street. Baba Kuda lived in Moffat Street, named after Robert Moffat, one of the British pioneers who had arrived in Rhodesia a few centuries before. Baba Kuda opened the door and greeted Mr Shoko with a big hug; they must have shaken hands for at least two minutes. There followed all the traditional ceremonial greetings that usually happen when two Africans meet: Mr Shoko and Baba Kuda addressed each other by their totem, asked about the well-being of each other's families and animals, the state of the weather and, lastly, the length of the journey. Both of the adults spoke noisily, and mainly at the same time, taking no notice of the small young girl, standing lost and tired by their side.

The house wasn't very well-lit; there was no electricity, and a single candle sat on the table in the middle of the room. I could smell food from the kitchen, which awakened my hunger and transfixed my eyes to the door of that room. When

I finally looked round the room I was in, I saw green plastic sofas from Nyore-nyore Furniture. One of the sofa's legs was supported by a brick. There was a wireless radio, switched 'off, and some Ever–Ready batteries lying around on the floor, probably as a reminder for Baba Kuda to replace them. I wondered where Baba Kuda's wife was, what she looked like and what Kuda himself was like. Would they like me? Where would I sleep? Before I could finish my thoughts, Mr Shoko quickly introduced me to Baba Kuda. I dropped down on one knee and greeted him very softly, shaking his firm hand. Straightaway, he gave me my very first assignment as the new house-servant: go to the kitchen and finish cooking supper. He then turned back to Mr ! Shoko, continuing their conversation without thinking to explain any details.

I went into the kitchen and saw a small pot crackling on the paraffin stove, almost to the point of burning. Inside the pot were small pieces of meat, and green rugare vegetables lay on the table, probably to be added to the meat. I fried the meat until it was crispy brown, then added some onions, green vegetables and, finally, tomatoes, with a pinch of salt and a cup full of water for gravy. I took out the best pot I could find in the cupboard - there weren't many, and most were either rusty, missing handles or had left-over food almost rotting inside - and started to prepare sadza to go with the sauce. I made double sure there were no lumps in the sadza, that it was cooked to perfection; the final results made me very happy because I knew I'd passed my entrance test to my new job as the family servant.

I went back into the sitting room and knelt down beside Baba Kuda, telling him that I had finished the cooking. It was a custom for servants to ask their employers to dish out the food they had cooked, especially when the sauce included a little bit of meat. Baba Kuda was pleased; he followed me through to the kitchen and started to dish out the food onto three plates. He left some in the pots, and asked me to bring two of the heaped piles of steaming food into the sitting room. I politely did as requested, then went back to the kitchen to fetch a bowl of water for the washing of hands. Our custom was that the eldest person was to wash their hands first; I knelt down next to Mr Shoko, then moved on to Baba Kuda. Things have changed these days; people no longer share the same water from one dish. A jug is brought round, with an empty dish and kitchen roll, and everyone takes a turn washing their hands individually without using the same water. This change has prevented a lot of diseases from spreading through the use of dirty water. These days, some people even insist on washing their hands in a sink with running water.

When the hands were clean, I took the bowl back through to the kitchen and quickly went for my plate of food. It had one piece of meat, a few vegetable leaves and a lake of gravy. I didn't dare open the pot for extra meat or sadza; I didn't want my new boss to think I was a thief or dishonest. I knew he had counted the pieces of meat that were left in the pot, and that he had instructed me to leave the leftover food for next morning's breakfast. I ate everything on my plate and still had room for more, but that was it for the day. After finishing the washing up, I was handed a blanket to sleep on the floor, and Baba Kuda and Mr Shoko went into the two separate bedrooms to sleep comfortably on their springy beds.

I was completely exhausted. I blew out the candle; the room became very dark, and an eerie feeling took over. The furniture seemed to start moving around. An unknown fear gripped me. I quickly covered my head with the blanket and wondered what the next day would bring. I was looking forward to meeting the lady of the house and the child that I was here to look after. Would I make good friends to play with? Back at home, my family's politics had stopped me from having too many. Anyway, I'd never had time to play; there was always so many tasks to be done, helping my mother with the never-ending housework. On most holidays, we would head out to the detention centre at Gonakudzingwa to visit my father. My chances of making friends in the village were never particularly good.

In one of the bedrooms, somebody snored very loudly. I decided to go to the toilet; there was no way I was going to wet the bed on the first day in my new boss' house. Please God, no!

CHAPTER 3

Baba Kuda woke me up early; it must have been around 5.30 a.m. I was still drowsy, and parts of my cheeks were covered with dribble. I tried to wipe it, but some had already dried and I felt uncomfortable caught in such an embarrassing situation by my new boss. I was shown to the shower and told to hurry up with preparing the breakfast; Baba Kuda was ready to go to work. In the bathroom, a long metallic pipe stuck out, with a tap attached to it and a round ring at the top that had tiny holes staring down at me. I twisted the tap; immediately, a gush of freezing cold water shot down all over me without any warning. I gasped as the water rained down; my whole body was frozen, my clothes were drenched and I felt miserable. Switching off this strange new shower, I splashed into the kitchen in my wet clothes and started to prepare breakfast. I lit the paraffin stove and warmed up the leftovers from the last night's supper. The smell was delicious; I suddenly felt very hungry! , but couldn't possibly risk my job by eating the boss' breakfast! Still, the heat from the paraffin stove helped to dry my clothes, making me feel a little more comfortable.

In the background, Mr Shoko was yawning - a sure sign that he had smelt breakfast and was ready to join the party. When they had finished eating, Baba Kuda thanked Mr Shoko for bringing me over and wished him a safe journey back to the village. He told Mr Shoko that, after work, he would take me to meet his wife and son. That was when I realised that my journey wasn't yet over; I wondered where I'd be heading to next. After Baba Kuda left for work, Mr Shoko hung around for a few hours, then, with a quick "look after the house", hurried back to the terminal to catch the twelve o'clock bus. I desperately wanted to beg him to take me back with him. I wanted to tell him I was afraid to stay in this strange house alone; that I was missing my mother already. Instead, I said nothing, other than to wish him a safe journey home. That was the last time I saw Mr Shoko for a long time. When we next met, it was during the war; he had become the chairman of the village, and I was to witness the terrible way he lost his life in the hands of the freedom fighters.

Left on my own, the house became very quiet. I was hungry and tired. There was nothing to do; I had quickly finished all the chores that Baba Kuda had asked me to do. I sat down and started to doze off slowly, sometimes jumping up at the sound of voices from outside, or cars passing by in the street. Finally, I slept. I dreamt of my brothers and sisters playing under our huge mango tree. Each of them had a juicy mango in their hands;

they were laughing and enjoying themselves. I tried to reach out for one of the mangoes, but one of my older brothers smacked my hand and everyone started to laugh. My heart broke; I could feel burning fragments inside, and cried with a deep and restless pain. I woke up, but the tears wouldn't stop. I told myself it was just a dream, but the pain of seeing my family from such a long distance was all too much. I sobbed quietly, then slept again, waking to a rumbling stomach and nothing to eat. I longed for Baba Kuda to come back, so I could at least start to feel normal again.

After another fitful sleep, I was woken up by a sound at the front door; someone was twisting a key in the lock. I froze, holding my breath, ready to scream. The door handle turned slowly and an image appeared at the door: it was Baba Kuda, and the time was now half past six in the evening. He was out of breath and looked like someone had chased him. He was obviously in some kind of rush, because he immediately told me to grab my bag and follow him to the bus terminal, where we would catch the seven thirty bus to Zhombe. While walking, he told me that his wife was a school-teacher at Zhombe Mission School and that his son was nine months old and was called Kudakwashe - "the will of God". That's all the information I received; not another word was passed between us.

At the terminal, Baba Kuda bought a bottle of Fanta and two buns for me. For the whole of the journey, he talked to some of the men on the bus about football and the latest local gossipy news from Mkoba and other local townships in Gweru. The big story was about some guy called John, who had been run over by a car near Mkoba shopping centre. Apparently, he had just left a prostitute's house and was rushing home to his wife in the early hours of the morning. After he had been hit, his wife passed by on her way to the vegetable market and saw policemen asking if anyone could identify the body. John's face was so mashed up that even his wife couldn't recognise him; she carried on to the early morning market in Mutapa Village. As chance would have it, John's prostitute was also passing along the same road to buy bread and milk with her latest earnings. She, too, saw all the policemen and the crowds of people, and she, too, was asked to take a look at the gentleman lying dead in the road. Stepping around the body, she asked the police if they could undo his trousers; reluctantly, they complied. As soon as the prostitute saw his crown jewels, she knew it was John from Mkoba! What a story that was! It even went as far as the news broadcasting corporation; soon, the whole country had heard about poor John's wife, and a lot of people sympathised.

We arrived at Zhombe Mission at half past ten, and walked through the darkness to the Mission School. Baba Kuda knocked at the door; I stood behind him, nervously looking around. The door opened and a tall slim woman stood there smiling. She was beautiful, with a light-skinned face but very dark legs. We went inside the house, which was well-furnished, with nice green sofas and a display cabinet full of glasses for wine. There was a Panasonic radio and a small black and white television with a clothes hanger acting precariously as its aerial. I was told to sit on the floor, and Baba Kuda and the woman sat on one of the big sofas next to each other. The woman was Mama Kuda; I was told to address her as "madam", and quickly realised she spoke very little of my mother tongue.

A child started to cry in the bedroom next door; Mama Kuda went in and came back with a little baby, who she instantly handed over to me. That was my introduction to baby Kuda. He was crying because his nappy was soaking wet; when I asked if I could change him, Mama Kuda pointed out a heap of clean nappies in the corner of the room. She seemed very pleased that I knew how to manage the baby on my own, with very little help; I had grown used to changing nappies at home, where I would often help out with my younger brothers and sisters.

Madam went into the kitchen and brought back some food for her husband. She told me that, as soon as the baby was asleep, I should go to the kitchen and have my own dinner. I quickly put Kuda to sleep, this time not in the big bedroom, but in the spare room, where there was a small mattress already made up for him. The room had no other bed, except for a reed mat and two thin blankets folded away in the corner. This was where I was supposed to sleep with the baby, whilst madam enjoyed the pleasures of the night with her husband. Not only, it seemed, was I due to look after Kuda during the day, I'd also have him at night.

Back in the kitchen, I found a plate with some sadza and a piece of meat on the side. I ate hungrily, and finished quickly, just before madam walked in with her husband's plates and told me to wash the dishes before going off to sleep. There was no sink in the kitchen, so I had to go out in the pitch-black night to do the washing up. There was no moon, and I could hear owls hooting not very far from the house. I could also hear madam and her husband laughing. I can't tell you how frightened I felt; I kept looking around, convinced that someone was about to attack me. After washing the plates as fast as I could, I rushed back into the house, put them away, went into the sitting room to kneel before Mama and Baba Kuda and thank them for the food, then hurried away to bed.

The next day started very early in the morning, when I was woken up by Kuda crying for his morning feed. As I tried to get up, I suffered the horrible realisation that I had wet my bed during the night, and that my clothes were now soaked in urine. The baby had also soiled his nappy, so the general smell was deeply unpleasant. I was very nervous, and hurriedly started to change my clothes and the baby's nappy. I was determined to cover my tracks by washing everything off before madam awoke. Unfortunately, my plan didn't work; as I turned round, heading towards the kitchen to prepare the baby's milk, I saw Mama Kuda already standing at the door of my bedroom. She had seen everything. Furiously, she told me to quit my stinking village habit of wetting the blankets. She warned that life would be hell if she caught me again. That was the first good morning I got from Mama Kuda. Her warning hit home hard. I was terrified; I knew the bed-wetting was something that I wouldn't be able to stop. This wouldn't be the last time; all I could do was get on with the job and pray for a miracle.

After finally succeeding in making Kuda's bottle from Lactogen powdered milk - my first attempt was so bad that I had to secretly throw the whole lumpen mixture away - I got the baby settled, and was told to take the dirty nappies and blankets down to the Mission dam to wash. I had no idea where this was; all I was told was to follow the path on past the school and I'd soon find it. When I did, quite a few people were already fetching water with carts pulled by over a dozen donkeys, which occasionally urinated straight into the dam. Some women were at the sinks, washing their clothes; I greeted them, but no-one replied. I later realised that they didn't speak the same language as me.

Quietly, I got on with my chores. Some of the nappies were so badly soiled, and had been kept for so many days without being soaked, that it was very difficult to work out how best to get rid of the greenish gangrene muck. Still, I did my best and, when all was done, carried the washing home on my head and in my right hand, with a bucketful of water in my left. Mama Kuda was waiting to inspect the washing. She didn't look at all pleased; not only did she think I'd taken too long, she also said that the results were unsatisfactory and that, next time, she expected the nappies to be as white as snow. I wondered how I would ever be able to produce such results; no detergent could really get rid of those stains, even if the nappies were soaked for a year!

After putting the clothes on the line, I was shown two big plastic drums - about 100 litres each - and told to fill them up with clean water from the dam. It took at least thirty trips to finish the task, each time coming back with a bucket of water balanced on my head and two more in each hand. My neck hurt so bad by the time I was done, but I didn't even have time to complain; the ironing was waiting, and I had to do it with baby Kuda on my back.

At half past eleven, I was given a rest for breakfast, which consisted of a mug of black tea and a crusty slice of bread, thinly spread with margarine. The rule of the house was that I wasn't allowed to eat any part of the loaf, except for the two crusty ends, and even then only one a day. I was to have no more than one piece of meat a day, with plenty of gravy or greens for my supper. Sometimes I would get the foot of a chicken, or the neck or the head. I used to hate seeing the head of a chicken staring out from my sauce; its unblinking eyes always seemed to be pleading with me to release it. I would always pick up the head and crush it, hoping to kill off my guilt. Lunch was never provided and, if any meals included fish, I was only allowed to have sauce. This would be my diet for over a year and half, as I struggled to satisfy the endless demands of a lady whose real name I never knew. I only ever called her madam, or, on rare occasions, Mama Kuda.

I started to cheat a little. When I was making the baby's bottle, I would make a little bit extra for me, quickly drinking it down before I fed Kuda himself.

Of course, I only treated myself like this when madam was busy at school, and I was alone with the baby. I looked after baby Kuda so well that there was a great improvement in the way he looked. Madam didn't suspect a thing; she simply thought that Kuda was drinking more and more. I started to do the same with the baby's food, especially Cerelac porridge. It was survival of the fittest, and I had to take my chances when I could.

Unfortunately, the bed-wetting didn't stop, so neither did Mama Kuda's beatings, which always tempted me to run away, even though I had no money for the bus and very little idea of the way back to my mother's village. I started to plan my escape; I didn't want to just run away while madam was at work because I could never have left Baby Kuda alone - he was the only true friend that I had in my imprisoned world. He used to smile at me, sometimes giggling so much that I ended up laughing as well. There was a special bond between us; we understood each other so well. He would scratch me for attention with his warm little fingers, especially when my mind had travelled to distant lands. I would look down at him and he'd smile back, his face lighting up like a candle and his little eyes twinkling like a star! He was almost like my own biological baby, and I never liked to see him upset. He was my little treasure, my little angel, who could bring me back from the darkest cloud and make me to feel human again. And now I would leave him forever.

I calculated the journey, thinking of nights I would have to spend in the forests, how long it would take, and how I could ever survive with all of the snakes, the scorpions and wild men. What would I eat? I meditated, and prayed to God for protection. Once more, I likened myself to an Israelite in the house of Pharaoh; I prayed to God to deliver me from this bondage. I often looked up to the sky for a sign; each shooting star bore the same wish: that, one day, I would be free, and happily returned to my family.

Mama Kuda's house was very big. She shared it with a colleague, Mrs Moyo, who was also a teacher. Mrs Moyo's husband was the deputy head, a giant of a man, with big fat lips and a belly that seemed destined to burst. Mr and Mrs Moyo didn't have a housemaid, so I was often called upon to work for them, making my tasks very heavy indeed. My knees were always sore, either from kneeling down when addressing my bosses or from polishing the red cement floors of the house. Everyone in the house spoke the same language, which I didn't understand at all. Sometimes, they even told me off in that language; all I could make out were a few oft-repeated words: mutakhathi, amasvina, inja, umusundhukanyoko. I later learned their meanings: dog, dirty Shona, witch, asshole. Of course, I already knew they were far from kind words; the beatings assured me of that.

I remember once, madam was yelling abuse and kept on encouraging me to answer her back; when I refused, she took a bar of soap, forced it into my mouth and rubbed it around until my saliva had started to foam. The smell of that soap stayed with me for a very long time; even today, it still holds a place in the back of my mind. When madam and Mrs Moyo were not at home, Mr Moyo would call me to the main bedroom and order me to hold him tight. He would grunt like a pig, making me squirm with discomfort, then his huge body would shake like an earthquake and he'd start to sweat, breathing so heavily I feared he would die. Sometimes, he would ask me to sit on his lap while I was holding baby Kuda; whenever I did, I would feel something very hard protrude from his trousers, causing me to shift over sideways. He would bark orders for me to sit still, or simply hold on to me tight until he his grunting was done. Then, with a stern look, he would warn me never to say anything to anyone at all; if I did, he would take me deep into the darkest forest and kill me and nobody would ever know. He told me he had killed before, and wouldn't hesitate to do so again if I so much as dared open my rotten mouth. These acts and threats became a routine part of my life. Each time, I was left with a sickening feeling and a growing awareness that whatever exercise Mr Moyo was taking, it was definitely something he shouldn't be doing with me.

By now, the thought of running away was occupying my mind so much that I don't even really notice half the abuse. I kept telling myself I was soon to be free, and my heart would dance with joy at the prospect of seeing my brothers and sisters again. In my head, I would sing all sorts of songs of freedom, and drown in the thought of breaking away from this misery and all of these people who remained alien and abusive to me. I was daydreaming so much that I sometimes burned holes in the clothes I was ironing. Luckily, madam never found out; she had so many clothes that she couldn't keep track of them all. Every Sunday, she would bring a whole bagful back from mass - second-hand clothes that were sent from Europe to churches in Africa, intended to aid poor families, but mostly ending up in the greedy hands of people like Mama Kuda. When I burnt the clothes, I would simply bury them in the bushy garden. I was never caught; not that it mattered; life couldn't have gotten much worse. I was totally unappreciated: a servant, of no interest to anyone in the house. I was treated as a scavenger; I was there simply to clean up their shit, to be spat at, kicked and abused; this was my reward for trying to do good. Not once did madam or anyone else say "thank you"; instead, I was constantly made to feel small, humiliated and guilty for all the hard work that I did.

My salary, I was informed, was being sent back to my family to help support my brothers and sisters. This was never the case; I later learned that my father, who never smoke or drank, had developed a terrible gambling habit. Whenever payments were delivered home, he would disappear for two weeks at a time, losing all the money at poker. Mother never saw any of my earnings, and those foolish dreams I'd had of driving a red sports came to seem like hideously misguided delusions. My only hope in life was to find a way to get back into education. How this could be achieved, I had very little idea. All I knew was that I missed going to school, and that even if it was only when I was a hundred years old, I would someday continue my education and reach a level that could allow me to develop my life. I was determined to rise above my tormentors. One day, I promised myself, I would even speak excellent English!

CHAPTER 4

Mrs Moyo came back from school one day with a young lady, about ten or twelve years older than me. This lady had a coffee-brown complexion, with short brown hair and the breasts of a nursing mother. She also had large cracks on her feet, which left prints on the ground like the wheels of a tractor. Her name was Sipiwe, and I was informed she would soon be starting work for Mr and Mrs Moyo. Boy, was it good to heat that; I was so happy and relieved that I almost broke out into dance. My workload, I instantly thought, would now be much smaller. What's more, I'd finally have someone to talk to, other than Baba Kuda, who I only ever saw once a month, and who would only speak to me when his wife wasn't around. Baba Kuda could see the sadness in my eyes, and I could see the guilt on his face. Not that he could ever change anything; the poor man feared his wife almost as much as I did. That's probably why he always looked so thin and malnourished.

Unfortunately, I soon realised that Sipiwe wouldn't be half the blessing I took her for; if anything, she only added to the nightmare. She couldn't speak my language, and it's not unfair to say that she looked down on me from day one. She never did her duties, unless madam and Mrs

Moyo were present, and she soon started bullying me badly whenever we went to the dam to fetch water. She took all the leftover food, insisted on telling almost everyone about my bed-wetting, and even stopped me from having a bit of baby Kuda's milk or porridge. The thought of running away increased everyday.

The final straw came one Sunday, when madam and Mrs Moyo arrived home from mass with bags full of clothes and a black catholic nun who went by the name of Sister Gabby, short for Gabriel. A big meal was prepared; two chickens were killed, and served with boiled cabbage and brown rice that I'd pounded myself. Madam used to buy sacks full of rice, still in their shells, and I would have to pound at least two gallons a day, with Kuda crying on my back. The first time, my hands hurt so badly with blisters that I struggled to wash Kuda's nappies. Naturally, this got me into trouble with madam, who continued to insist on them being as white as snow.

After the feast, everyone stayed out on the veranda, enjoying the last rays of the sun. They each had a bottle of Fanta, and were listening to a variety of songs chosen by listeners to a radio show called Kwaziso - "Greetings". How I longed to hear a message of greetings from my very own family! Sipiwe was told to play with Baby Kuda, while I took out the dishes to wash, but Kuda refused; he still wasn't used to Sipiwe. Kuda loved to go on my back; I would tickle him and sing lovely lullabies. He especially loved the one I'd learnt at school that went: "Sleep, baby of mine, the jackals by the river are calling, soft across the dim lagoon...". In the end, I did the dishes with Kuda on my back, hoping to gain a bottle of Fanta as a reward. Wishful thinking, once more; when everything was done, Mama Kuda simply said that, as a bed-wetter, it wasn't good for me to take fluids in the evening! I looked round at everyone and saw no signs of shame or pity in any of their eyes, except, perhaps, for Sister Gabby, who seemed concerned. She didn't say anything, but kept on looking at me at the expense of the conversation.

It was only after she'd left that the bags of clothes were brought out. Most were claimed immediately by either madam or Mrs Moyo, but there was one colourful dress, pleated with pink roses and made of a velvety material, that was just my size. It was the prettiest dress I'd ever seen and I instantly forgot the whole Fanta incident as madam lifted it up and passed it across to Mrs Moyo, who was sitting right next to where I was kneeling down. Mrs Moyo commented on how pretty the dress was, how unfortunate that it wasn't their size. I gazed in anticipation as she reached out to me with that wonderful gown. My hands were open, the dress came right by my fingers, so I could feel its velvet, enjoy its colours, and then it flew through my grasp and fell in the hands of Sipiwe.

At that moment, my heart felt as if it would explode into a thousand fragments. I was so humiliated and hurt; I can't even remember heading to bed, where I sobbed uncontrollably the whole of the night. I prayed and recited psalms, just as I had as a little girl at Sunday school back in the village. How life had seemed so simple and sweet. I knew I had to run away.

The next morning, I woke up very early; it was still almost dark when I started to carry out my never-ending tasks. Mama Kuda and Mrs Moyo seemed surprised, but didn't say a thing to acknowledge my effort. By start of school, I had already finished most of my morning duties; all I had left to do was wash my wet blankets and baby Kuda's nappies. Sipiwe was now up, and was acting like a princess with her beautiful new dress. I ignored her to start, but she kept on coming right in my face and calling me names like "bed wetter", "smelly", all kinds of nasty things. She said the reason I hadn't been given the dress was because madam and Mrs Moyo didn't want it to be spoilt by the stench of my urine. But when Sipiwe finally tried on the dress, she found it didn't fit her round the chest and was too short. I laughed sarcastically; she instantly slapped me right across the face, followed up with a sharp, stinging kick to my buttocks. I fought back; pretty quickly, Sipiwe was down and I clutched at the beautiful dress she was wearing. As she pulled herself up, there was a loud ripping sound, like a rusty zip; the pretty velvet dress was torn. Sipiwe was left wearing the top half of the dress, and I was holding its skirt. She came charging towards me like an angry rhino, swearing she'd kill me. She would have had to; I'd taken so many beatings, that I was fully prepared to fight to the death. I waited for the chance to grab her face, then dug my teeth into one of her cheeks, splattering blood over what was left of the dress. Sipiwe started screaming, and ran towards the house. Some school-kids who were watching the fight rushed back to alert our bosses. I was left alone, spitting blood, with murderous thoughts all over my face. I'm not afraid to admit I could easily have murdered Sipiwe that day.

Mama Kuda and Mrs Moyo came rushing back from school. Mrs Moyo was already swearing and madam was waving her hands in the air; I knew there was bound to be big trouble and prepared myself for further beatings. Mama Kuda came straight over to me and slapped me so hard that it felt like the whole left side of my face had been submerged in hot cooking oil. My ears buzzed as if a thousand crickets had invaded my head. What followed was beyond any form of beating I had ever witnessed or felt; by the end, they were kicking a lifeless doll. Only God knows how I did not die that day. Only when blood was pouring from my mouth and nostrils did they finally stop. Some of my teeth were wobbling; the rest of my body was numb. Looking up from the blood-stained dirt, I saw Mrs Moyo gently nursing Sipiwe's swollen cheek. They were practically cuddling. Did nobody care about me? I was an unwanted, unloved soul; nobody heard my cries. Even God had turned his back. What was the reason for me being born in the first place?

Mrs Moyo promised Sipiwe she would sew the dress back to perfection. She had a Singer sewing machine, and would even add extra material to make sure the dress fitted better this time. It gave me some comfort that, by the time she was finished, the dress looked nothing like as pretty as it had. Mrs Moyo had added a different kind of material, taken from her husbands khaki shorts. The dress was reduced to a horrible cloth - one of the ugliest gowns in the world; I would never have picked it up in the street. God certainly works in mysterious ways!

Anyway, Madam and Mrs Moyo went back to school to resume their duties; I was left with a whole heap of new tasks to perform as part of my punishment. Sipiwe was simply told to lie down and avoid any form of work. Naturally, *she* was hurting, and apparently still in shock. Some people are just lucky, full stop! I saw my chance for freedom, and was determined to flee as soon as my two bosses had disappeared behind the trees. I would leave my lovely baby Kuda with Sipiwe, and she would end up much busier than she now thought.

I went into the bedroom, where I slept for a while before collecting my few belongings in a little brown bag. In the kitchen, I cut a big chunky slice of bread and stuffed it in my bag. My heart was pounding like a drum for fear of being caught; at least it showed I was recovering sense after the numbing beatings. My body was stiff and tense; at times, I could feel an intensely sharp pain in my ribs, as if someone was stabbing me. Ignoring the pain, I carried on with my mission. Fortunately, both baby Kuda and Sipiwe were sleeping; I could hear them snoring heavily. With a quick last glance round the room, I tip-toed to the door and left the house.

As soon as I was outside, I started to run. The pain gripped me hard, I was sweating with fear, and my stomach was making loud noises as if thunder had entered my body. I hurried on regardless, not looking back once until I was at least four miles from the Mission School. Finally, I started to breathe a bit deeper, sucking the air in but unable to reduce my fear. I was determined to walk as fast as I could in order to get through the approaching forest before it got dark. There were rumours of hyenas, and wild men who would abduct young children, selling them on to superstitious businessmen who would kill them and use their blood for a magical potion to increase their profits. Some would only want your heart; some, the whole of your head. I didn't know what to fear most: the hyenas, the wild men or Mama Kuda!

In a very soft voice, I started to sing my old Sunday school songs. I still jumped at the sound of each broken twig; sometimes, only the sound of my feet was enough to urge me on; I could have sworn it felt as if someone was following. The back of my head was freezing cold, as if I had no skin or hair. Still I sung those old hymns, especially "Guide me Oh thou Great Jehovah". I was an Israelite, about to cross Jordan into Canaan. I saw the shadow of God, covering me in protection. As I was swallowed up by the forest, I felt an overwhelming sense of His presence. I pictured God as a magnificent man, with a great white beard almost down to His knees, shining like polished silver. I grew bold with the thought that I wasn't alone. This God that I saw would never seek to destroy anyone; to me, He was the gentlest man that I'd ever encountered. I felt comforted, and didn't realise how far I'd come until I was heading out of the forest's darkness.

Aside from God, I hadn't met a single person along my way; the only sounds I'd heard were the cooing of doves and a few distant booms from the chests of baboons. As I emerged out on to the road, I got scratched by some bushes and stubbed my foot painfully on an unseen sharp stone. One of my big toes was already bleeding, and the nail had almost come off, but this was no time for self-pity - I still had to find shelter for the night. By now, I was extremely tired and hungry. I finally remembered the chunky piece of bread buried among my clothes in the little brown bag.

In the distance, about a mile away, I could see Mr Dube's store. There was a river in between; I knew that after crossing it I was bound to meet people either going to or coming from the shop. I stopped singing, and ate all the bread quickly. At the river, I scooped up its water, salving my dry throat with almost two pints. I climbed the road to Mr Dube's store, went straight to the veranda and sat myself down. Boy, was I tired, and had no idea what to do next. The sun was already setting; soon it would be dark. I watched the last flickering golden rays; they seemed to be winking at me, and a great warmth enveloped my body. Everyone seemed to be hurrying around, desperate to take advantage of the last of the light. I just sat quietly on the veranda, remembering how, in my family home, we always had to find enough wood for the fire. No one wanted to be outside in the dark for fear of scorpions or snakes, or old witches, riding around on hyenas, but we needed the fire to roast our dry maize, and to watch grandmother's face as she carried on with her endless folk stories. Some of her stories were so horrifying that we had to huddle together in fear. Perhaps we simply wished to be close on those cold winter nights.

I never enjoyed the warm nights as much; I was always told to sleep outside of my as a result of the whole bedwetting business. I dreaded those mornings when I would wake up in urine and everybody would call me names and hold shut their noses to avoid the stench. I would hang the blankets to dry on the line round the back of the kitchen. By the end of the day they would have roasted, becoming as hard as if they'd been starched. They were like knight's armour; I slept in blankets as hard as rock.

Once, when it was my brother's turn to bring in the wood, he forget until it was very late and the fire had almost died down. As he rushed outside in the dark, we could clearly hear his footsteps behind mother's hut; he was making so much noise that probably everyone heard. We all laughed at his cowardice. He came back quickly with a few logs in his hands, but before he could even put them down there was a loud scream from my sister. We all stared at my brother's shoulder, frozen on our ox-hide mats. A snake, balanced on one of the logs, was curling up towards his face. When he realised, my brother threw all the logs of fire on the floor, including the one with the snake. I can't begin to describe what happened next. Everyone scattered like mice, all screaming and forcing their way out the door. Somehow, big old grandmother managed to get out first, despite her bad back and dodgy legs. The snake chased us out of the hut, then when we were out, it chased us back in, so that we ended up almost falling into the big pan of popcorn and groundnuts.

Our neighbours, who had heard the noise, came running to see what had happened. The big man next door arrived with a knobkerrie, but the snake had already disappeared. No one wanted to search the dark grass; instead, we ended up with a full house of neighbours, sharing our popcorn and groundnuts and grandmother's stories. This time, she told us a nice romantic tale, not wanting to frighten us any more than we'd already been. My sister had even wet herself with fear; she was very quiet for the rest of the night and I felt sorry for her - I knew exactly how she felt!

As I perched on the store veranda, remembering days gone by, Mr Dube, the shop owner, simply carried on with his tasks. After a while, he came out from behind the counter and started to speak in the same language as Mama Kuda. By now, I'd mastered a few words, and politely tried to make myself understood. When Mr Dube realized I was struggling, he started to speak in my mother tongue, which was a tremendous relief. To hear someone speaking my language felt like a ticket to freedom; at that moment, I realised just how much I missed my own family and how very far I was from home.

Mr Dube asked me to come into his store. My heart skipped with fear as I stood up slowly to follow him. Inside, the dark shop smelt so strongly of bread and oranges that I was attacked by some unannounced hunger pains, nibbling away inside me. Mr Dube turned and smiled. He had gaps in his teeth. For the first time, my face looked directly at his. What I saw was a very dark man; dark to the extent of being almost too black. He was simply as dark as the night! His face was as ugly as a hippopotamus, and his lips were so huge and thick I could have sworn they'd been turned inside out. What had I done? I felt like crying or running or calling for help; my legs were like concrete. I was convinced that Mr Dube was one of those terrible businessmen who slaughtered young girls for good luck. I was so scared, I hardly even noticed the voices that called from outside; it was only when they reached the veranda that I turned round to face five big boys from the Mission School. Mr Dube let them in, and they told him the whole story.

"Take her home", he said. "I was about to do it myself." He closed the doors to his store; he didn't look at me once.

The boys led me back to the School, slowly at first, but at a much faster rate as we entered the forest. I ran alongside, not because I wanted to return, but because I had no choice; I didn't want on spend the night with wild animals in the forest, and there was no way I was going back to Mr Dube's store on my own. Something about him had really given me the creeps.

It was now very dark; the moon only occasionally popped out from behind the dark clouds to light up our way. This time, though, I wasn't afraid of the forest; they might have been primary school pupils, but the boys were big - easily old enough to have their own families. Such was the way; because of strict government laws, which insisted that black children could only move up if they passed all of their subjects each year, it was very normal to see older boys and girls still at school. Often, students only left school to start up a family, sometimes with one of their teachers! My eldest brother fell victim to these oppressive laws; he had already secured a place at secondary school and was about to begin when a white Education Welfare Officer discovered that he had failed one of his grade seven subjects. He was directly expelled from the school, even though he had successfully completed year eight.

We finally reached the Mission School just after midnight. When Mama Kuda opened the door, the boys instantly disappeared. Pulling me by the ears, she shoved me into the bedroom, kicked me and went off to fetch Kuda, who was crying louder than I'd ever heard. All he needed was a change of nappy.

CHAPTER 5

It was early one Sunday morning that Mama Kuda informed me, in not so many words, that I was about to be sent home. Apparently, I'd become too much of a risk; not only had I kept on running away, but my weight had also dropped down so badly that you could count every bone in my body. I looked like I was living in a drought-stricken country; my skin had grown as dry and wrinkly as an old lady's, my head was bald from carrying endless buckets of water, and my hands were as rough as sandpaper, thanks to all the bleach that I used on the nappies and all the sand that I used to scour the pots. Baba Kuda had decided it was time for me to leave, and I would join his return trip to Gweru.

It's hard to express my relief. I felt like a prisoner who had just finished a long jail sentence and was now finally facing her freedom. Inside, I sobbed with joy, thanking the Lord for looking after me. I even thanked madam and everyone in the house for their kindness. No one said a thing. I gave baby Kuda a mighty big cuddle and took him outside to sing his favourite lullaby softly in his ears. My eyes were filled with tears.

It didn't take long to pack my bag; there wasn't much to go in it. Soon, Baba Kuda and I set off to the Mission School to catch our bus, which came as soon as we reached the station. As usual, there was a lively crowd on board, carrying all kinds of food and animals to sell at the market. At first I got a seat next to Baba Kuda, but I soon gave it up to an elderly lady and stood up for the rest of the journey. Not that it mattered; I would have hung on to the back of the bus just as long as it led to my mother's.

We arrived in Gweru around half past three in the afternoon, then hurried off to Baba Kuda's house, where I hurriedly prepared some food for our dinner - Baba Kuda was soon to start his evening shift at the shoe factory. The house was much the same as the last time I'd seen it, except the chairs were more worn and some of the pots had gone mouldy with leftover food. I went outside to the sink and washed everything thoroughly before lighting the paraffin stove, which was covered with food and grease.

By the time Baba Kuda had finished his shower, dinner was already cooked and the smell of sadza and fresh greens had filled the house. Baba Kuda reached up to the cupboard and brought down a tin of corned beef, which he asked me to add to the green vegetables. Corned beef - what a privilege! I had difficulty opening the tin; I'd seen plenty before, but madam had always insisted on opening them, so I never got a taste of that special meat that looked so smooth and smelt so sweet.

Corned beef, so I was told, was only meant for well-respected people, like madam and her family. One day, when I was taking an empty tin outside to throw away, I'd cut my finger on its sharp corner as I poked round for a lick of the flavour. Determined to not let madam know what had happened, I stuck my bleeding finger in my mouth and tore a small piece of cloth from my tattered dress to bandage the wound. Unfortunately, Mama Kuda noticed the cut and made me confess. She then gave me a great telling-off, calling me "scavenger" and all sorts of names, before ripping open the bandage and pouring fine salt directly onto my wound. I almost passed out, but Mama Kuda just laughed and loved every minute.

It was with this in mind, that I cheerfully opened Baba Kuda's corned beef and liberally dished it out. The brown meat smelt so good that my mouth instantly filled with saliva and I could literally feel my taste buds tickling. I was in corned beef heaven! As I held out the dish for Baba Kuda to wash his hands, I told myself that this was the last time I'd have to kneel before this man. I went back to the kitchen and ate like there was no tomorrow. My luck, it seemed, had finally changed.

As soon as Baba Kuda was finished eating, he set off directly for work, pausing only to show me how to lock the door and find me a candle for the night. With the door firmly locked, I finished the dishes and got ready for bed, thinking to myself how Baba Kuda seemed a bit kinder than the rest of his people. Perhaps he only wanted me to seem in better health when I greeted my parents, but I couldn't gain weight in a day and, no matter how nice he was now, my body told a miserable story. I went to bed with two blankets, one on the floor, and the other for cover. Lying there, I couldn't help wondering what my family would do when they saw me. Would they be angry, happy, anxious relieved? With questions running through my mind, I somehow fell asleep.

The next morning I was woken up violently by a loud bang on the door. Baba Kuda was back from work. Before opening the door, I peeped through the window and was surprised to see a lady with big platform shoes, bright red lipstick and a very short skirt accompanying the man of the house. The woman was wearing an afro-wig, all very curly and black. Her face was orange but her legs were dark. I noticed she was slightly taller than Baba Kuda, who she kept on calling "darling", much to my confusion. According to the way I knew things, you only called someone "darling" if you were married to them, or at least going out. It was certainly a sign of intimacy.

When they entered the room, I stood quiet and polite; Baba Kuda may have been cheating on his wife, but I was still only a servant! He told me to pack up my clothes; we would soon be heading for the terminal to catch the twelve o'clock bus to my village. I thanked him for his kindness, even thanking the lady as well, though I had only just met her. As we were leaving, the lady with the afro-wig reached out to Baba Kuda and kissed him full on the mouth. I quickly looked down at the floor; I had never even seen madam do that to her husband. When I looked up at Baba Kuda's face, his lips appeared to be bleeding with lipstick, which was smeared up the side of his cheek. I couldn't bring myself to say anything; after all, he was my boss and this "darling" sideshow was none of my business. I looked away again, laughing oh so quietly to no one but me. When we set off for the bus, we left the lady in Baba Kuda's house. She seemed very much at home.

"Good for him!", I thought to myself. "With a wife like Mama Kuda, the man deserves a little bit of happiness - he's only human for goodness sake!"

My bus was already parked at the terminal with a few people waiting inside. I felt a pang of excitement as I quickly spotted some familiar faces from the village. It was real; I was finally going home! Freedom at last! Baba Kuda paid for the ticket and gave me thirty dollars to take home to my parents. The rest, he said, would follow after pay-day. He handed me two plastic bags; one with four loaves of bread, a pack of margarine and a big tin of jam, the other held a huge cabbage, a small bottle of cooking oil and a kapenta fish, with its squashed little eyes peeping through the plastic. I thanked him and waved goodbye. That was the last time I saw Baba Kuda, or any of his family.

The bus was packed; I couldn't move my feet. Some drunks were singing songs to encourage the driver to go a bit faster. Whether their trick worked or not, it was three o'clock when we arrived at the village and I alighted at Mr Mangai's bus stop. On the right was Mr Muruvi's house, then the Zungura home, the Gungurukwa's, then my parents'. I was nervous. I felt almost like an intruder as I walked slowly and softly towards my mother's hut. No one was around; the home was deserted except for the chickens, which roamed the yard, scratching the ground for maggots and a few invisible crumbs. I peeped through the door of the hut. Beans and corn were cooking in a large clay pot. The family must be somewhere nearby! Pushing open the kitchen door, I lay down my bags, checked the pot on the fire, and then decided to go look for my family in our garden, down by the Zhovoringo River.

On the way, I met a good few locals, all heading back from the river after washing clothes or watering fields. My family, they told me, were still down in the garden. Some of them laughed, and made comments I couldn't catch, but I paid no attention. I simply wanted to see my family. As I slowly approached our garden, I glimpsed my mother standing, clutching her back. Only when we were close up, face to face, did she realise who I was. By then, I was crying, and she started, too, almost screaming in a loud and painful voice. My brothers and sisters came running from the river. Their faces were etched with surprise and confusion. It was clear that no one had been expecting me.

Mother was heavily pregnant; her tattered blue dress couldn't cover her stomach. She asked us to close our eyes, then she prayed to God, thanking him for returning her child. On one level, it was like I'd never been away; I was soon helping the others to finish their chores, before we went back to the house where our dinner was waiting. Yet I found it hard to fit back in, struggling to communicate with my brothers and sisters. I must admit, I was resentful of their obvious happiness, and annoyed by my exclusion from their little games.

The thirty dollars I gave to mother; she showed it to my siblings, and later gave it to father, who threw it all away on gambling. Despite working hard, and trying my best to make friends in the village, I soon came to realise that things had irrevocably changed. I was no longer regarded as a young girl by my peers, who saw me instead as an adult. Indeed, it was in adult society and life that I seemed most useful; despite my discomfort, I had no choice but to start to behave like a grown-up. Otherwise, it seemed I would be out on my own.

When I came back to my family, I had expected to continue my education, to live a normal child's life alongside my brothers and sisters. This was not to be the case. Perhaps it was pure negativity on my behalf that stopped me enjoying life back at home in the village. All I felt was pain and isolation; I could only see myself as an outcast. What hurt the most was that no one would trust me; people called me a liar, or ugly, or all sorts of nasty names. I came to deeply resent myself and hate the way that I looked, especially my teeth, which people said looked like a warthog's whenever I smiled or laughed.

Each night, as I struggled to sleep, I could only think of the misery of the next morning, when I would invariably end up carrying my wet blankets down to the river, where a dozen other girls would always be waiting to laugh.

"Wait," they would always say. "Let us finish our own laundry first. Don't pollute the river with your smelly urine. Your acid is killing the fish."

CHAPTER 6

It was the season of fruit; fresh foods were growing all over the orchards. Wild sweet fruits could be picked from the forest, or fresh maize from the garden, or pumpkins or star fruits or melons. The moon shone so bright at night. Boys and girls would come out to play, singing and dancing to the rhythms of the African drum. Bigger boys and girls would hunt for love, sneaking off to bushes to steal kisses or share brief but romantic cuddles. Frogs could be heard for miles, croaking, calling out for rain and mates. The old owl would hoot from the big fig tree, or swoop through the village, from hut to hut, preying on mice and rats. It was rumoured that witches could feel through its claws when its eyes lit up like small fires. The whole world was at peace. Happiness could be seen in the sky. Shooting stars shot past one by one.

Unfortunately, I was among the very few people unaffected by all this beauty. Oh, I was very much aware of it, and I really did try to appreciate it. But I could never shift the nagging sense that there was something in my way, something stopping me from fully sharing the season with others. In truth, I was sad and lonely. I still didn't feel like part of the family. I would lean on the walls of my mother's hut, wishing on stars for an escape from this misery. Most of all, I longed to be loved, appreciated and respected as a human being. I would sing softly until tears reached my mouth and I licked at their salt. I had no friends in the village, despite my best efforts to help anyone who ever needed an errand. In fact, I was treated little better than a village donkey; perhaps my slavery days were not over just yet.

Once again, I started to questioned God's purpose in putting me on this earth. I needed a net to catch myself, or a ladder to reach my desires. I needed to learn about this thing that people called "love", what it felt like to have and to give. My spirit was empty. I was numb to everything around me and, probably, some of the attention given to me passed unnoticed with me lost in my miserable thoughts.

Whenever I was with my family, someone would make a joke and I would try to laugh along. Instantly, always, I was reminded how ugly I looked, how my exposed teeth made me look like a pig or a hog. At other times, I would be told there was something wrong with my nose; it was too small or too flat, or maybe my complexion was too light. People played with my name, twisting it from Mina to Maina. I grew to hate it so much that I would always hesitate to tell anyone who I was. When I did say my name, I would quickly look down at the ground, avoiding all eyes and hiding the pain on my face. I came to believe I was the ugliest girl on the earth, and that I would never be of any worth to anyone, no matter how hard I tried.

Big men in the village would make sexual advances, and random older women would expect me to do their chores. My brothers and sisters would sometimes help, but that never stopped the pain that hung over from my time back in Zhombe. Perhaps it was me; I had closed every possible avenue to allow my family to express their love. Maybe I feared that, if I ever opened up, I would only end up enduring even more pain and rejection. Fear had become the story of my life. Sleeping was now a nightmare; the bedwetting lasted. One man in the village had got into the habit of exposing himself each time that he saw me. He would wait by the path to the river, knowing I would never tell, for fear of being branded a liar. As I was coming to realise, sometimes people just don't appreciate the truth, especially when you tell it straight to their faces.

Around this time, my mother's sister and her husband often turned up at our village, picking up fresh fruit to sell at a market back down south where they lived. They drove an open truck, which we would always fill up with food. Sometimes, they would treat us to a ride round the village on the back of the truck. But never when it was full; we couldn't afford to squash all the fruit. Our journey home would always be made by foot.

My mother used to make the best meals for her sister and brother-in-law. Each time, they would bring us margarine and tins of jam, bags of sorghum and rice, and at least half a dozen loaves of bread. It was Christmas come early. My aunt and uncle were the richest people I'd ever seen; I couldn't help but admire them. On one occasion, they brought their lovely daughter, who was just a touch taller than me. She was beautiful and slim, and always wore pretty clothes. I was a couple of years older, but she always seemed so grown-up.

One day, I decided to take her to the river for a swim. Secretly, I wanted to show her off to the village girls who refused to play with me. Instead, I got the biggest disappointment of my life. When we reached the river, six girls from the village were already preparing to swim. As they took off their clothes so did my cousin without hesitation. I stared at their naked bodies and instantly knew I was different. They had pubic hair, and breasts sticking out of their chests. I didn't have either; only an overwhelming desire to run back home. I was uncomfortable, inadequate, with nowhere to hide and a growing sense of being stared at. They started shouting at me to take off my clothes; my own cousin was the first to guess out loud why I wouldn't. When I did - slowly - they all laughed, and threw pebbles at my shapeless body. I edged downriver, away from their taunts, and spent the whole afternoon on my own, watching my cousin chat away to the girls as if she'd known them all her life. She even told them about my bedwetting, and that I was a liar and ugly.

When I headed home, soaked and ashamed, it was with a broken heart. My mother was sitting with her sister by the big mango tree, eating all sorts of fruits from a big reed basket. When she asked me where I had left the "baby", I was completely confused; could she really mean my cousin, who was almost a grown-up? When I said she was still at the river, playing with the other girls, I was told in no uncertain terms to go back and fetch her. This I did, but only after mother had called me inside of the hut, away from the eyes and ears of my aunt, and handed me a big slap round the face. I ran back to the river, dazed, and ordered my cousin to come back home. We didn't talk the whole way. Even the next day, we still weren't speaking; I simply avoided her until she left with her parents in the evening. When my aunt promised to return in two weeks, I sharply resented her wealth. It made us seem like slaves.

The next time my aunt and uncle came, it soon became clear that fruit wasn't all they would take. This time, they had come for me as well. Apparently, this had already been discussed with my family; it was agreed that I would be of great help to their eldest daughter, who had a one-year-old baby and was now pregnant again with another. I would also be of great support to my cousin, who was on her own and struggling with her studies. We would go to school together; my mother, it seemed, had already got a letter from the local school's head accepting my transfer. We would be in the very same class, so that I could offer the utmost support to my cousin. This, of course, meant that I had to redo a class I'd already completed, spending a whole year learning topics I'd already covered and passed. It was disheartening, but I knew that I had little choice. Perhaps, I thought, this could be an escape from my lonely existence, and from the dirty old man that still followed me down to the river. All I could do was pack up my bags and hope for the best. I was given a brand new blanket - grey, with stripes on the both ends; it almost looked like a rainbow. My aunt took thirty dollars to pay for my fees and school building fund. This money, I was told, had come from Baba Kuda as the last payment of my salary. At least someone had finally kept a promise.

That very night, I said farewell to my family and set off in my uncle's truck. He hadn't paid his road tax, or licence or insurance or MOT; unsurprisingly, he was somewhat scared to drive in the daytime. Only one of the truck's headlights was working, though, and even that one was fairly temperamental, so my aunt had to hold up a big torch, which added to the powerful moonlight. I was excited to be riding in the front seat, where I sat on my aunt's lap, squashed in against the door. The truck had a radio, so sometimes aunt and uncle would cut off their chatter to listen out for the news or a nice song by Miriam Makeba, the South African simanje-manje diva.

After a while, I was told to jump in the back of the truck, and my new blanket was thrown in to cover me. My aunt issued a stern warning that I shouldn't pee on the fruit, but, within a few miles, I'd grown bored of counting the stars and fallen asleep. The next thing I knew, my uncle was shaking my leg, and a good few people were loitering by the side of the truck. It must have been about one o'clock in the morning. I immediately recognised my cousin, and soon guessed that the others were her two sisters and brother. On my right was a big yellow house with a beautiful veranda. My uncle called out to the hut on my left, and two girls and a tall young man instantly appeared. These must have been the workers or servants.

As I stood up to get out the truck, I felt a terrible cold trickle come running down my legs. I had done it again; I had wet myself and some of the fruit was covered in urine. Everyone saw it and started to laugh, except for my uncle, who angrily ordered me to go behind the house and wait for a worker to bring me some water. Only after I'd washed would I be allowed inside. As I walked round the side of the house, I wished that the ground would swallow me up. Of all the times to wet myself, why did it have to be now, on my very first night in my rich relatives' house?

After washing with very cold water, I was finally shown inside. Everyone was getting ready for bed. I was taken to one of the smallest rooms, full of tools and spare truck parts. There was a mat and two blankets, one of which I had brought myself. I spread them out, lay down and covered my shivering body. With my knees curled up to my chin, my hands tight between my legs, I soon fell asleep once again.

I was woken up early to start my first assignment of the day. Sister Veronica arrived with the baby, who was already crying for her morning feed. I had to call her my sister, as was the custom; your mother's sister's daughters were also your "sisters", her sons, your "brothers". It felt better than calling her "madam"; perhaps I could pretend I was part of the family, rather than feel like a slave.

With Veronica pregnant again, it fell to me to prepare the baby's bottle. I was soon left with the wailing infant and a few basic instructions about where I would find the bottle, nappies, washing basin and all of the rest. Veronica also told me to bring her a cup of tea in bed; apparently, she had a bad headache and her blood pressure was a little bit high. I later discovered that Veronica's "headaches" were just a way of getting what she wanted and that nearly everyone in the family had their own special illness for that very same reason. With the baby already in my arms, I struggled up and painfully realised that I'd wet my bed once more. Luckily, by now I was both an experienced bed-wetter and an exceptional childminder. I held the baby on my damp back, folded the wet blankets, then headed to the kitchen to prepare the baby's bottle and her mother's tea.

The kitchen was big, with a large coal stove and chimney. I hadn't yet learnt to use such a stove, so I decided to learn on the go. I opened its door and pulled out a tray full of ashes, causing the baby to sneeze. At least she was no longer crying; I'd quickly changed her soaked nappies and she was now snuggling on my back, almost asleep. Some logs had been cut into blocks to fit into the stove. I picked a few of them up, arranging them nicely on the bottom of the oven before topping them with newspaper and a second layer of logs. Then I took a match and lit the fire. At first, there was nothing but smoke, but after a few minutes I saw result of my efforts: I had successfully managed to light a coal stove without any guidance at all. I filled a large black can with water and brought out a small saucepan for the baby's milk. After rinsing the baby's bottle to wash away a strong smell of sterilising tablets, I filled it with milk and made

Veronica's tea. I then washed the baby, splashing plenty of Vaseline blue seal on her velvet-smooth body. I even squeezed a bit of Johnson and Johnson's baby powder on her bum, making her smell all nice and fresh. To calm her hiccups, I administered a touch of Gripe water, which some adults would use to cure heartburn.

By the time this was finished, everyone in the house had woken up and rushed to the stove one by one for warm water to wash their faces in preparation for breakfast. Labourers were already at work in the house's large garden, some weeding, others planting fresh vegetables. The world had come to life again, and early morning birds were struggling to catch worms in the freshly-dug ground. My aunt seemed very pleased with my efforts; she said I was like her own daughter and that I should address her as "mother". My other three cousins - Beatrice, Tracey and Bobby - were also now awake. Bobby was now my "brother", and the other three my "sisters". Their father would be my father now, too.

Tracey was the youngest, the one who had visited during the season of plenty. I could tell by her looks that she didn't appreciate my efforts at all; she seemed to think I was just showing off. Beatrice, on the other hand, didn't take much notice of me; she simply brushed by on her way to the stove. As soon as father arrived on the scene, he instructed me to go to the garden and join the workers in whatever they were doing. I would be called for breakfast at the same time as them. Leaving the family as they prepared a nice breakfast - eggs, stewed meat and lots of bread - I walked out to the garden to greet my new colleagues.

There were eight of them, and they had divided the duties neatly between them. My task, I was told, was to carry the grass and pile it in heaps for the compost. Some of it was extremely prickly; by around mid-day, when we were finally called for tea, my hands were all sore and itchy. Our breakfast amazed me. There were no eggs, no meat, and not even much bread. We were each given one slice of bread and a single cup of tea. That was all. It was at this point I saw beyond the family names, the "sisters", and "brother" and "mother". I was not a part of this family; I was just one of servants - end of story! I should have been used to this heartbreak, but it came once again as I shock. I felt trapped, isolated, with no way out and no one to defend me. I was an unloved, unwanted soul, numb with pain. Had I been cursed on the day I was born?

My afternoon task, according to Veronica, was to fetch water from the dam and wash the baby's soiled nappies. I had been here before. My other two sisters were lounged out in the sitting room, listening to romantic European music and devouring comics and magazines. I soon found out that Beatrice liked "Teddy Pendergrass", Bobby, "Rose Royce", and Tracey, "Abba". For my part, I was simply happy to hear any kind of music, even from a distance and even if I didn't have a clue who the singer was.

After washing the blankets and nappies, I proceeded to make my sisters' beds. I took some wild flowers from the garden and arranged them nicely in an empty jar beside their beds. My feet were now throbbing, but as soon as I sat down on the veranda I was handed the baby again by Veronica. Words were said to the effect that my big bum looked such a comfortable resting place that the baby should always be put on my back whenever she cried or was due for a sleep. While I was to be with this family, it soon became clear, my duties would never end. I soon learnt to get on with my tasks without waiting for instruction. I was also a comedy act. Whenever the family felt like a laugh, they would put simanje-manje music on the record-player and call me to give them a dance. They would get me to do "a-go-go", or "wee-shu", then laugh until they could barely breathe. Naturally, I didn't find it amusing at all; in truth, I felt degraded but saw no way out - this silly routine at least gave me the chance to be social, and avoid more tiring tasks. Soon, I was even formulating new moves, or dancing with the baby on my back. It was tiring, and humiliating, but also the only time that I ever felt like a part of the family.

I didn't mind doing the dance; at least I was close to some sort of human interaction. That was good enough for me.

Across the bridge from the house of my aunt lived my grandmother - my mother's mother. She was an elderly devoted Christian, and lived with her daughter and some of her grandchildren. Their father had gone off to Europe, apparently to study, although we were later told it was down to political reasons. Their mother had died. Personally, I wasn't very close to the children; I never got the chance to get to know them. Grandmother's youngest daughter - the one that she lived with - was unmarried with three children. Grandmother hardly ever crossed the bridge to visit her wealthiest daughter, despite the fact that she struggled to get by and the only support she got came from a son who owned a shop in the south of Zimbabwe.

Speaking of shops, there were a couple of stores just over the bridge towards grandmother's house. One of them I particularly liked to visit; there was a boy there called Melvin, who worked behind the counter and who I quickly developed a crush on. He was the son of the store-owner, Mr Marshall, and he used to give me free drinks, which I'd gratefully accept before rushing back home and rubbing my mouth clean so that no one would know what I'd done.

Soon, it was time to start school. My sisters and I had been registered at a local school, two miles away from the house. The route lay along two straight roads, one made of tar, the other of gravel. There was a short cut, but it involved diving through gardens and fields, climbing dusty tracks and crossing a small river. I was excited by school; it was where I belonged. When classes were done, I always wished for the rest of the day to disappear, taking us straight to the start of the next one. I wore black tennis shoes and one of Beatrice's old dresses. My uniform, so I was told, would be ordered at some later date; there had already been an apparent mix-up, and Tracey was now in possession of two new uniforms, as well as nice shiny shoes and a brand-new school bag. The explanation was that one of the uniforms was supposed to be mine, but that father had forgotten I was a little bit bigger than Tracey. This was something I soon grew used to; every time new clothes or shoes were bought for the children, no one seemed to be able to remember my size.

On the first day of school, I woke up as usual to prepare breakfast: a fried egg and plenty of bread for Tracey; a crust and some tea for me. This time, I also had to make Tracey's lunch, which consisted of a bottle of Fanta Orange and a packet of biscuits. There was nothing for me; I was simply supposed to wait for Tracey to finish her food and then ask if she had any leftovers. After all, she was the baby of the house, so she obviously had to eat first! As you might well assume, Tracey never left much for me; she had lots of hungry friends at school and didn't feel like sharing with one of the workers. I hated being in the same class as her, but there was nothing I could do.

On that first day, I was unfortunately late, so Mr Dube, the fierce head teacher, made himself known with a powerful beating. Mr Dube was very dark with a short round neck and an amazing grasp of the English dictionary, especially given the fact that he had only ever completed grade six in his academic studies. Even for simple instructions, he always used extremely big words, which we nicknamed "jaw-breakers". Despite the confusion his words inevitably sowed, Mr Dube managed the school exceptionally well and had a very good supply of teachers. The school even had decent textbooks, so there was no excuse for me not to study well. I made a vow that I would break the school record by getting top marks every time. I loved my books and valued the chance to go back to school so much that even the lack of lunch didn't annoy me. After all, I was far from the only pupil to go without biscuits and juice. Two of Melvin's sisters were at the same school, and I was soon happy to discover that they liked me more than Tracey. Sometimes, they would bring extra food from their store, handing it to me away from Tracey's icy glare.

My class teacher was brilliant; very beautiful and well-educated. In fact, I think she was probably the best teacher I've ever come across in the course of my life. Her name was Miss Sibanda. It meant, she once told us, the sun, the moon and the stars, and if anyone deserved such a name it was her. She gave me the most valuable education of my life, even if it was only at primary level. Through her, I learnt how to be bold in life, and how important education could be for a girl. I think her confidence and ability even intimidated Mr Dube; he knew she deserved his position, but even she was unable to overcome the male domination of power. Still, she was my inspiration. She saw a vision of my future before I ever could. She told me to never give up. Slowly but surely, we became good friends and I started to confide in her, telling her all of my troubles. For some reason that I now forget, a few of us came to call her Miss SV. She seemed to quite like it; I guess it made her feel a bit different, a bit special and unique.

When I was just about to move up to secondary school, Miss Sibanda married my brother Bobby. It wasn't an easy relationship; Miss SV was never liked in the family home. She was quickly branded a witch and a whore, and would later be held responsible for Bobby's death. I, too, would take a large chunk of the blame. After all, it was I who had introduced them; how could I have not known that she was a filthy prostitute!

Under Miss Sibanda's wing, I grew to be one of the brightest students at school, if not in the whole of the province. At home, though, life was becoming unbearable. Veronica was now living with her husband at his workplace. They had been given a big house in a remote part of the city, about twenty-five kilometres away. It was always very difficult to find transport to Veronica's place, and coming back was even harder. Veronica's husband had a motorcycle so it was easy for him to travel around. He was an agricultural inspector for the whole of the province, which made him very well-known and respected. Veronica herself was now training to become a home economics supervisor; she had little time to look after the two young children, so my assistance was needed every weekend and throughout the school holidays. I was always in demand. When I wasn't child-minding, I'd be selling freshly cooked maize in the townships, or working at Bobby's music bar.

At weekends, I would wake up early to walk the four miles from our home to the city. From there, I would hitch-hike to Veronica's. Sometimes I would walk all the way, arriving around five in the evening to find Veronica angrily and instantly ordering me off to the dam to fetch water before it got dark. There were rumours that the dam, or even the whole area, was haunted. The story went like this: Veronica's husband had been married before, and had murdered his wife during one of their regular fights. Her spirit, it was said, had never gone away, and she was often seen in the evenings or early mornings, stumbling around, crying for her young children. Veronica once told me that, in the silence of the day, she could sometimes hear a female whisper asking to enter the house. She said that, if I ever heard that voice, I should ignore it at all costs.

I never did hear that voice, though I also never overcame my fear of the house. It was such a big house, and I was expected to clean it every day, polishing the surfaces until they shined like mirrors. When that was done, it would be time to feed the babies, or perhaps wash their nappies. Strangely, I was almost the most scared when I was left all alone with the babies. I never knew whether to sit outside on the big veranda or lock myself safe in the house. Whenever one of the babies cried, I could feel myself starting to sweat and hear my heart beat as loud as a drum. My body would always go numb. Things always got worse when I heard the sound of Victoria's husband's bike. He always came home drunk, holding a briefcase in one hand, a fresh loaf of bread in the other. He was a very tall man, and was known as the family medium; he often used snuff and carried the name of one of his ancestors as well as his own. Whenever he arrived home before Veronica, he would call me over to collect the loaf, then reach out and fondle my breasts. I didn't understand why he did it. One day, he called me to his bedroom, where I was startled to find him undressed. He just laughed, and said that if anything ever happened to Veronica, I would become his new wife. I was stunned with embarrassed, then quickly walked out of the room. He called out after me, sounding pleased with himself and warning me of what would happen if I was ever to tell anyone. Soon, I had a reason to hate him even more: I discovered he was beating up Veronica nearly every day.

Around this time, I often had to work at Veronica's allotment, weeding the groundnuts and maize. It was about two acres big, and the grass had grown so high that it was difficult to pick out the crops. This naturally slowed me down, and my hands would always be covered in blisters by the time I got home. I was continually tired, what with one task after another, but there was never anyone to complain to; not even my own parents came to visit like they'd promised they would. I used to pray for the school holidays to end, so I could go back and talk to Miss Sibanda.

Selling freshly cooked maize was far from an easy job. Father would count all the maize in his truck, then divide it all up into four piles: one for Tracey, who had her own spot in the market, right next to her daddy's truck; the other three for the female workers and I, who were constantly moving from street to street with steaming-hot dishes of maize. We would make a round ring of cloth to put on our heads, then sit the hot dishes on top. Each of us was given a dollar's worth of loose change in a small sling bag to help out the customers. When one plate was bought - for twenty-five cents - we would hurry back to the truck for another. Sometimes, father would drive round and find us, handing us more platefuls of maize and checking we were doing our job. Of course, we were never allowed to spend any money, no matter how hungry we grew. We weren't even allowed to eat maize. When the day was done, father would do what he called "stock-taking"; if even a single penny was short, it would be docked from the workers' wages. If he thought I was to blame, my chances of going back to school with new tennis shoes or new pants were instantly lost. The only way I could ever make any money was by cheating some of the oldies out of their change; through this route, I was sometimes able to save enough money to buy myself buns or a Fanta.

By now, the hair in the middle of my head was beginning to break quite a lot, to the point that I had developed a small patch that was visibly bald. When I went back to school, teasing quickly grew so vicious that I resorted to crushing black charcoal from the stove and mixing it with Vaseline to rub on my head. This didn't really cover the patch, but did put people off from trying to touch it;

when anyone did, their hands would get smeared in black grease, and others would start laughing at them instead of me for a change. Eventually, nobody bothered.

I was a very good netball player at school and became a member of the first team. This didn't please Tracey, who, unsurprisingly, grew jealous and wanted my role. I was very passionate about netball; I even borrowed clean knickers from friends whenever there was a serious match. Mine were all old and tattered and torn. I was also in the school choir, which was taught by Miss Sibanda. She was a great musician, and she taught me how to read scales; we used to learn how to sing songs in notes before she ever gave us the words. Music classes were an absolute pleasure; how I wished they would last forever. School was my fortress, my one place of freedom. I was now in grade seven, and doing exceptionally well. But it couldn't last.

One Sunday evening, sometime during the Easter holiday, I was at Veronica's house, working the weekend as usual. I had finished my chores and was getting ready to go home; by now, it was around five o'clock and I'd already said my farewells to Veronica and her husband, who were sitting on the veranda enjoying the last rays of the sun. The babies were sleeping; I'd fed them and washed them and left them looking contented. I had two hours to get into town before father left for home from his shop. If I didn't catch a lift with him, I'd be totally stuck, so I started to run down the path. When I reached the main road, I was already almost out of breath. A few cars passed by; I stuck out my thumb, but they barely acknowledged my presence.

Finally, after a two-mile walk, a car pulled up and a man in a suit, all professional-looking, asked me to where I was heading. He told me to hop in, and immediately drove off at such a fast speed that I practically fell on the dashboard; I had to cling on to his shoulders, and the car swerved a little, but the man only laughed and turned up the radio. I was just starting to relax when the man took a sharp turn along a narrow strip of road that only seemed to lead to a forest. I asked him where we were going, and if I could get out of the car, but he just kept on driving, looking dead straight ahead and never saying a word. His face had now changed; something was definitely wrong and, to make matters worse, we were approaching a notorious mountain where not many people ever went; those that did would rarely return.

As the driver turned up the music, I told myself that now was the time to take action. I reached over to the passenger's door and opened it quickly while the car was still moving. Jumping out, I landed brutally in a bush nearby, rolled downhill for a few painful seconds, then hauled myself up and ran off, with the man now out of the car and charging in pursuit. He threw stones, then stopped, and the next thing I knew there was a loud crack of a gun and a bullet flew past me.

By now, I was screaming and running as fast as my legs would allow. Only when I was right at the top of the mountain did I finally stop, hearing the sound of the man's car driving back to the main road. I started to walk back down; it was growing dark and fear had gripped me hard. I stopped at every sound: a snapping twig, a bird flying past. Sometimes, a lizard would whisk through the grass. I would stop, hold my breath, look around, and hurry on. When I finally saw some lights from the city I felt so relieved that I instantly fell down to the ground and praised God. I cried and cried; when I rose up, my dress had been badly torn. I just kept walking. When I reached the main road, I headed back towards the market, turning a corner to see father's car driving past, with everyone sat in the back. I shouted and waved but nobody saw; at that moment, I felt my heart break into a thousand pieces.

There was nothing else to do but walk faster; there was still a chance I could catch him at the market. My prayers were soon answered; just as father was about to restart the car, there I appeared, knocking at his window. He switched off the car engine and started to shout: why had I left Veronica's place without waiting for him to collect me? Why was I so silly and stupid? I just stood there and took his abuse, crying openly until he eventually realised something was wrong; I had never shed a tear around him before, despite all the beatings and scoldings. Still angry, he asked me what had happened, and I gave him the story between sobs and apologies; I hadn't known he would come and collect me. He told me to jump in the back of his truck, and said that he would report my story to the police the next day. That was the first and last time I heard him talk of the story; the only change that came out of all this was that he started dropping me off at Veronica's on! Fridays himself, and her husband would now take me home on a Sunday - naturally after pausing a while to fondle my breasts. Sometimes, he would stop twice, once just after we left, then again just before we arrived. How I dreaded those horrible trips in his car!

Back home, I grew increasingly isolated, and threw myself into my studies. My final exam was approaching, and it called out to me like a promise of freedom. I was completely determined to pass, reading each book from cover to cover, reciting everything I'd learnt and asking myself questions out loud. In the mid-term examinations, I had come top in all my subjects, closely followed by a boy called Dickson, who was always frustrated to lose out to a girl. The only time he was number one was when I had to miss school for two weeks because of chicken pox. He still only beat me by two points, but nothing could stop him from celebrating as if he'd won a jackpot. He laughed at me, too, and I was so annoyed with myself that I cried all the way home, vowing never to lose my position in class ever again.

Tracey, for some reason, always came bottom or second-to-last, despite all the advantages she had. The family never took my school results seriously; they clearly thought that Miss Sibinda was favouring me, and that she was probably telling me the answers to each question paper, even though it wasn't even her who wrote them. I was desperate to prove everyone wrong in my finals; these exams were not set at our school; they came all the way from the capital, Salisbury (now Harare). On the day of the exam, I prayed for God to give me the wisdom that King Solomon had had in the Bible. At breakfast, people kept asking me to do this task and that; I knew it was part of a plan to discourage me, but I swore not to let it affect me.

When the exam was over, everyone started excitedly chattering about which secondary school they hoped to move on to. I was aiming to go to a boarding school; it seemed the quickest way out of my misery. The bed-wetting still hadn't stopped, and I still spent my nights in the tool room. One day, just as I was getting ready to go to sleep, my uncle had walked in and said something about some electric wires that were lying on the floor by my bed. I hadn't heard him clearly and assumed that he'd asked me to move the wires out of the way. As I touched them, a huge ball of fire immediately blew up all around me; I was thrown to the wall and blacked out. When I came to, I was lying on the veranda, surrounded by all of the family, with my uncle desperately trying to force a Fanta bottle down my throat as part of his improvised first aid techniques. My aunt had been crying, and as soon as I opened my eyes everyone started to clap and laugh hysterically.

This wasn't the only time we suffered electrical dangers. My uncle loved to fix up old cars; he filled up the house with all kinds of welding machinery and metal objects until it came to resemble a scrap yard. He even had a generator, which used to supply electricity to the house via a whole network of unreliable wires. Things would often burn or blow up, but my uncle refused to give in. My aunt, meanwhile, grew distractedly angry as she continually tripped on the wires and banged into the metal.

When the exam results were published, I had passed with flying colours; in fact, I was one of the best students in the whole of the province. I had put my school on the map and felt on top of the world, especially because I'd been able to disprove all the nasty suggestions that the family made. I was simply a genius, full stop! Unfortunately, Tracey hadn't passed the exam; she had actually failed every single subject and, though she didn't seem bothered, I actually felt a bit sorry. By this point, she was always full of mischief and had become a bit of a handful to both of her parents, even though they were at pains to deny it. Beatrice, meanwhile, was going out with an Asian man who owned a business in the city. She definitely had her fair share of men.

I was still infatuated with Melvin, and he was head over heels in love with me; I knew this for a fact because he'd sent a whole stream of letters through his sisters. His parents liked me, too; when they heard about my final results they gave me a big present of assorted biscuits, a bottle of raspberry squash, two loaves of bread and a bottle of Fanta that came straight from the fridge. My family, however, seemed in no mood to celebrate; no one so much as congratulated me. Father took my certificate for safe-keeping and promised to look for a school, but finding a suitable place for Tracey was now central to all their concerns. Father apparently had contacts and was trying to organise something with his money and influence. Probably, he would bribe the principal of some secondary school into accepting Tracey despite her results. I guess that's why Tracey never seemed bothered; as far as she was concerned, all my hard work was a waste, my achievements a joke.

There was now only a month before school would re-start, and I still hadn't registered; in fact, all talk of me finding a good secondary school had died down. Instead, I was to be enrolled in a so-called "upper-top" school as part of a new government scheme to cater for those who had not done so well. The main subjects were domestic science, woodwork, gardening and sewing.

At first, I couldn't understand why father wanted to reduce me to this. Then it became clear: the school was close enough that I could commute; I would still be around in the evenings and weekends to take care of the endless and thankless household tasks. My school fees would be paid through my contributions over the holidays and weekends. Once again, freedom had flown out of my grasp; I was devastated, but told myself to keep going with what I had; beggars, after all, can never be choosers. Unsurprisingly, my school certificates had now disappeared; when father accused me of hiding them, my reminder that he was the last person to have them brought me a terrible beating. Without the certificates, there was no way I would be registered at any school; Tracey, it seemed, would have to take my place. This must have been part of the plan, because after Tracey was registered, my certificates soon turned up at Veronica's house; how they got there, nobody knows, although I once again took the blame.

It was around time that my mother's brother visited us from the Low-veld area where he was working. He arrived when we where almost in bed; I was in my little room, lying on the floor, contemplating ways to escape. There was instant excitement; everyone was keen to chat to Uncle Peters. When he mentioned my name, I heard them all fall silent. Finally, father told him where I was sleeping, quickly followed by some excuse concerning the room I was in. Footsteps came heading my way, and Uncle Peters was soon poking his head round the curtain that served as my door. He was obviously shocked by the state of my room; my blankets were torn and smelt strongly of urine; strips of cotton hung off them like spiders' threads. Peters just looked at me pitifully. When he went back to the sitting room, he demanded to know why I was kept in such appalling conditions; by this time he was openly crying and refused to accept any of the numerous explanations his sister attempted. !

That night, Peters refused to eat with the family; the next morning, he left straightaway to return to his workplace. Before leaving, he came into my room and secretly gave me a ten dollar note, telling me to follow him the very next day on the bus. The excuse I would give was that, since I hadn't succeeded in getting a place at school, I was best off with my brother Brian, who was now living with Uncle Peters and working as storekeeper for a Greek man called Tarso. Peters told me exactly which bus to take, and said I should tell the conductor that I was going to Mr Peters who had a shop at Tsobani Township. All I needed now was to gather the courage to say my farewells. As soon as Peters had gone out of my room, I drew back the curtain and knelt down to pray, with the ten dollar bill still clutched in my fist.

CHAPTER 7

I quickly did my chores, making sure there were no mistakes, then slowly walked out to where mother was sitting underneath the big guava tree. I knelt beside her, and told her my plans; looking into her eyes, I could tell she'd already guessed what was happening. Maybe Uncle Peters had even told her. Anyhow, she actually looked quite relieved, and reassured me that she would soon tell her husband and the others.

Father didn't take it so well; he went mad when he found out the news. He turned on me, shouting "this is what happens when you give a dog too much milk - it bites you when it grows strong". He said I was like a silly cow, kicking the master who was trying to pull out a tick from its back. Maybe he was right; I couldn't care; nothing mattered to me now except grabbing this new chance of freedom. With mother pleading my case, father finally gave in and allowed me to go. No one thought to ask if I had any money for transport, and I spent the whole evening alone. I was told to pack my belongings in my old plastic bag, and bring everything into the front room for an inspection - they didn't trust me to leave without stealing some family property. I did this, then put the bag by the door to pick up in the morning and went to bed for the last time in the tiny tool room.

That night, I dreamt I was in paradise, eating and drinking and looking happy and beautiful. I was with my real family, and laughing so much that I ended up waking myself up from the dream. I instantly realised that even now, on my last night in the house, I had again wet the bed. I can't say how disappointed I felt; I'd been planning to take the blankets with me. I now had no choice but to leave them behind, unwashed and stinking of urine. Mind you, I couldn't help but smile at the thought of Tracey, or maybe her mother, cleaning my blankets the following morning; this was my last chance to fight back, to avenge a small part of the misery I'd had to endure in the two and half years that I'd lived in this house.

I fell back asleep, then awoke to prepare for my journey. I went into the kitchen to fetch cold water for my morning wash, but was surprised to find all the cans and containers empty. I even looked in the tank for the stove; that was empty as well. I couldn't understand how all the water could have got used up overnight; it had never happened before, and on this occasion I definitely didn't have time to head down to the dam. There was no way I would risk missing my bus; I'd just have to go without washing.

I walked to mother and father's door, knocked gently and heard voices inside. I called out to say I was ready to leave. No one answered; the voices fell silent. I repeated myself, this time thanking them for looking after me; still no one responded. I got up from where I was kneeling and went to pick up my bag. I looked round the house for one final time, then closed the door quietly and started walking away. Tears were flowing down my cheeks; I felt rejected and unwanted and useless. I had no shoes on, still stank of urine and had sleepy dust all in my eyes. At least the tears helped to wash off some dirt. As soon as I'd closed the main gate, I started to run, crossing the small bridge and heading in the direction of Mr Marshall's store. I was happy to see that Melvin had just opened up; the smell of fresh bread entered my nostrils as I grew close to the store. I couldn't bear the thought of leaving without saying a final goodbye to Melvin and his sisters. He didn't seem at all surprised to see me; apparently, Tracey had already told him, or at least that she'd made up some story about me being kicked out of the house because I'd been stealing and generally causing trouble. Thankfully, I knew Melvin would never believe such a story; I felt no need to explain and simply thanked him for his kindness and asked him to pass on a message to Rosin and Janet, telling them how I'd miss them. Taking my hand, Melvin pulled me a little bit closer and gave me a kiss on my unwashed face - actually, right on my lips. His kiss was so tender and sweet that it both reassured me and made my heart beat fast; no boy had ever kissed me like that before; Melvin was one in a million. To kiss me like that when I was so smelly and dirty - the boy must surely have loved me! Before I left, he told me to write to him, and that he would await my return, when he would make me his beautiful bride. I wanted to stay there with Melvin forever. He gave me two bottles of Fanta Orange and a big pack of biscuits then led me quietly out of the store. On the veranda, Melvin caught sight of my unwashed feet and realised I wasn't wearing shoes. He ran into the store and came back out with some old rubber slippers, which were torn on the heels. They were a bit big, but I gratefully took them; I put them on; we said goodbye; I hurried off down to the bus.

By the time I'd reached the main road one of the slippers was already giving me a bit of problem; these new golden slippers, it seemed, were not destined to last me a day. Five people were waiting for the bus; I joined them, keeping a distance. After what seemed like forever, the bus finally arrived and we all jumped aboard. I was so happy to take my seat, finally assuring myself that this was it - this was my freedom - and no one could take it away. Except, perhaps, for the conductor; I wasn't really sure that I had enough money, so I hurried to the back of the bus to make sure he checked me the last. Back there, I'd be able to tell him what Uncle Peters had told me to say. I'd also immediately realised I was different from the rest of the passengers; everyone else looked as though they'd made a particularly special effort to clean themselves up. I was ashamed of my scruffiness and wanted to hide from their view.

As it was, by the time the conductor came for my fare, we had already passed five stops and were a good few miles from where I had boarded the bus. I pulled out the ten-dollar bill and quickly explained the whole story. Luckily, everything worked out as planned; the conductor told me not to worry; he lived next-door to Uncle Peters in the township and would make sure I got there safe. Any extra fare would be recovered later; perhaps he would ask Peters to finally fix his old radio.

We passed through the mine town of Mashaba, where my father's sister lived on a farm, then Chibi and Masvingo, home to the celebrated Great Zimbabwe ruins, where my father had been working when he first met my mother, before reaching Triangle in the Low-veld region, centre of the sugar industry. The bus moved at such a tremendous speed that it was impossible to look out the window without feeling sick. Music was playing loud and the journey grew increasingly tiresome; I came to feel as though we would never reach my destination.

Peters lived in a town called Chiredzi, named after the local river and very close to a big national park called Gonarenzou - "the place of elephants". As we headed further and further south, all kinds of people got on the bus; accents, even languages, changed. Locals started speaking Changani, a tongue as old as the Stone Age. Some of these newcomers were almost as scruffy as I was; this made me more relaxed and, after finishing both bottles of Fanta and the whole pack of biscuits, I eventually fell asleep with my head on the plastic bag that held my clothes.

When we arrived, the conductor tapped me awake. The bus had stopped at a busy market place, and the conductor confirmed that this was Tsobani Township, where my uncle worked. He also said he would take me to Peters' shop, so I picked up my bag and followed him out into the street. I suddenly realised my slippers were missing; someone must have taken them while I was sleeping. Not that it bothered me; I was certainly used to walking barefoot. There were a few little shops round by where my uncle worked, as well as a big supermarket called Taguta that had a restaurant and a clothes department too. As we entered Uncle Peters' shop, everyone stared. Peters himself was at the back of the shop fixing radios, and didn't realise we'd arrived until he heard the conductor speak; he then raised his head, put down his tools and came rushing towards me with arms outstretched. He was crying and laughing at the same time. After a few minutes of greetings and wiping away our tears, Uncle Peters remembered himself and thanked the bus conductor for bringing me home. How I prayed that this would truly be my home! Peters closed the shop and, holding my hand so tightly that it seemed he was scared of letting me go, he led me to his house at 297b Chademana Road. I had never known so much love in my life, especially not in such a short time; I would never have thought that anyone could be so kind to a child who wasn't their own.

Uncle Peters was like an angel sent from above; he was so very, very different from anyone I'd ever known. He loved a good joke and would laugh until tears flowed down his cheeks. He loved football so much that he would regularly travel to Salisbury to watch big teams like the Dynamos, Caps United and the Highlanders play. Back then, footballers might not have been paid as much as they are today, but they still carried celebrity status. Over the radio, on Rhodesia Broadcasting Corporation airwaves, you could hear Evans Mambara almost dribbling the ball with his comments. You could close your eyes and feel the ball hit the net. - that's how exciting it was! Some of our popular players were better than Beckham and Pele put together; people like Moses Chunga, Madhinda Ndlovu, David Mandigora and the ultimate goalkeeper Bruce Groblaar! The sound of a packed Rufaro Stadium would boom through the radio; the African drums would cheer all the way.

Uncle Peters also loved women, and, being tall, handsome and fairly well-off, he was never short of partners. He ended up with a few dozen children, which was never a problem in our culture. When we arrived at Peters' house, I was introduced to his wife, a beautiful young woman who must have been about seven months pregnant. My grandmother was there, too, and Beulah, my mother's youngest sister's daughter; even my own sister was there in the house.

Seeing Naomi was the icing on the cake; the last time I had seen her was when she was leaving for Mashaba to live with my father's sister, where it was planned that she would become her uncle's second wife. Apparently, Naomi had refused the marriage and been sent back home to my parents; as a punishment, our father had thrown her out and banned her from ever returning. She had then come to live with my brother Brian and his wife Nellia, but because Brian didn't have a very big house it was agreed that Naomi would spend the nights at Uncle Peters, which wasn't very far away. My sister had put on a little bit of weight since the time I'd last seen her; she looked very happy and much more mature. I was desperate to see Brian and especially his wife, who I had never met before. To be surrounded with my family, in a place of warmth and friendship, made me feel at peace; that night, for the first time in weeks, I didn't wet the bed. In fact, that was when it stopped for good; I trained myself to wake up at night and use the toilet instead.

On the morning after my arrival at Uncle Peters', Naomi woke me up and, together, we quickly cleaned the house, then walked down the road to our brother's. Brian was very happy to see me, and so was his wife, who was holding a small baby girl. Family bliss: it seemed all my prayers had been answered. I felt as though I'd fallen deep into a wonderful dream, from which I hoped I would never awake. This time, I quietly but confidently told myself, this time my freedom would last.

Those few happy days were spent with Naomi, Brian, his wife and my uncle. Sometimes, we would stay up to the early hours of the morning, listening and dancing to music, or amusing each other with tales and jokes. Peters and Brian were a proper double act - much like the Two Ronnies I would know in another life to come. It was such fun to hear them together, telling their never ending jokes and spreading their silly stories; those were probably the most memorably happy times of my life. I quickly became part of a netball team in Tsobani Township; we used to travel as far as Triangle and Masvingo to play other teams. I didn't manage to start school, though; I needed a letter of recommendation, which, unfortunately, never arrived. The principal of the local secondary school promised Peters that I would definitely be allowed to join the following year, with or without the recommendation, and I was happy with that; after all, I was free, and could finally see a future I liked. At the weekends, we would go to Tambuta Hotel Lodge with Naomi and her new boyfriend Sebastian. He would always bring a lot of picnic food, and we would sit by Chiredzi River, enjoying the breeze as we munched on our goodies and finished them off with a cold fizzy drink. On Sundays, after church, we would go to the local stadium to watch football. On the best days, Brian would be playing, and we would cheer his team with delight. Those were the days when I finally made my own friends, people who wanted to play with me, who were happy to laugh, dance and share with me. I started to feel like a human, like I was loved. I began to put on weight, and became so rounded and pretty, with the best complexion I'd ever achieved.

It was at this time that I first got to know my Aunt Jodie, who was a well-known woman and a fantastic ballroom dancer. She used to spoil me rotten, dressing me up in her prettiest dresses, but nothing could hide the air of sadness that hung round Jodie like a cloak. She was a very hard-working woman; she had never been married and, though she tried very hard to fit in with the family, they never appreciated her as much as they should have done. Maybe she was trying too hard. People gave her all sorts of names, but I liked Jodie a lot; I felt comfortable with her and, although she was much older than me, I could easily relate her story to mine. She was low in energy and confidence, and the men she still hoped to settle down with would only end up beating her until she lost half her teeth. One day, perhaps people will understand Jodie better, and perhaps she will understand herself better, too. No matter what, she'll always have my respect and my love; for a short while, at l! east, she helped make me a very happy young woman; she taught me to smile, and I'll always be grateful for that. Jodie used to tell me I was just as beautiful as anybody else. If only she'd been able to believe that about herself.

CHAPTER 8

One Friday afternoon, Naomi and I were passing by Peters' shop, planning to pop in, say hello and hopefully leave with an ice cream. A woman was sat outside the shop on a suitcase; as we drew near, I suddenly realised that it was my mother. She was holding a bottle of Coca-Cola, and on her right were my two other brothers and my baby sister Tombana. Naomi and I ran towards mother and jumped in her arms, knocking her coke to the ground in excitement. I hadn't seen her since I'd left home for the south to live with her sister. She was looking worn-out; maybe the journey had been very tiring, or perhaps she had brought bad news with her from home.

In my last year down south, Miss Sibanda had started inviting some of the older pupils to her house during the afternoons. This was all very hush-hush; I'd known that something strange was going on, but had no idea what. They would always prepare a lot of food, and I'd see them carrying it up to the big mountain at the back of our school. Miss Sibinda would lead this small group, leaving the rest of the pupils, myself included, with instruction to work or enjoy the freedom. It was a strange situation, and I grew increasingly suspicious, especially when Miss

Sibinda would go to the city with the head teacher, returning with a whole load of drinks - some alcoholic - that were then carried up to the mountain. On these occasions, the chosen pupils would never leave at the same time; instead, they would quietly depart one by one every five or ten minutes.

One day, I plucked up the courage to ask one of the girls, Eunice, what was going on. Taking me aside from the others, she whispered something strange in my ears about "comrades". Apparently, these "comrades", or "brothers", were all around us; all the smuggled food and drink was for them. Eunice warned me not to tell anyone. If I repeated the story, she said, not only would I be killed, but my whole family would perish! Naturally, I promised to keep it a secret; whoever these new brothers were, I certainly didn't want to upset them.

While we were talking, I kept thinking of a visit that one of my father's cousins had paid to our family home. He had come from the Gokwe region where he worked as a miller. As he sat in the kitchen having dinner with us, he'd told my parents how terrorists had come one night and set fire to the grinding mill. They had burnt the mill down because it belonged to the local white farmer, and these terrorists apparently hated white people. My father's cousin had gone on to explain that he had come back to ours because his village was now under curfew; the Rhodesian Army were hunting the terrorists, and no one was allowed to go outside after six. Surprisingly, my father seemed to enjoy this story; every time that his cousin explained something that made the terrorists sound truly terrible, father would raise up his fist and salute with excitement. I couldn't work out why he would celebrate over what sounded like such a horrible tale. I didn't yet know that these terrorists, or "magandangas", as they were often called, were young black men and women fighting for the liberation of our country. It was only that afternoon, when my mother appeared outside Uncle Peters' shop, that the full story was finally revealed.

The war, according to my mother, had now become very hot; lots of people were dying in our village. She had brought my brothers and sister to a safe place for protection. Walking and hitch-hiking, they had ignored the curfew and steered clear of main roads, which were now closed due to landmines or ambushes from both "comrades" and the Rhodesian army. Mother said she had been sent to collect me; I was needed to help serve the freedom fighters alongside other girls in the village. Uncle Peters protested strongly on my behalf; he questioned my mother on how and why the freedom fighters even knew I existed. Why were the other children being brought to a safe place, while I was to be sent back to face the horrors they'd escaped? Mother had few answers;

her explanation was that other girls in the village had mentioned my name and that father had expressed his desire that I should come and fight for the cause. If I refused, the freedom fighters would destroy our family home and kill all my relations, including my father and mother. I had no choice but to pack my bags and prepare to go home with my mother. I must admit: a part of me was excited and curious; I wanted to meet these so-called freedom fighters who were struggling for our liberation; but I was also scared. Once more, a new era in my life was beginning; I was entering the eye of the storm and, from here on in, there would be no turning back.

The next day, I said my farewells and spent the night dancing and packing. Mother and I woke at half-past six to catch our bus to Masvingo; from there, we walked or hitched lifts to Chibi and Cha-cha-cha because all of the bus routes had closed. The journey was very tiresome; my feet began to blister and I started to limp. The ground was as hot as burnt ashes, and we were unable to rest because people had been prohibited from offering comfort to strangers under any circumstances. Suspicions were growing, and fear was now written on faces. If either the Rhodesian Army or the freedom fighters were to stop us, we faced the very real threat of being beaten, or even shot; with this constantly in our minds, we travelled as fast as we could, looking around us continually.

My heart, so recently brimming with joy, had once again filled up with fear. I had reverted to a vulnerable child, with heavy responsibility weighing down my young shoulders and no real hope for the future. At Cha-cha-cha, we were lucky enough to find a tractor that was going our way; the driver said he would take us to Mbiri, so we hurriedly jumped on his trailer. We arrived, covered in dust, in the late afternoon and, after paying the driver, began the long walk to our home. Mother and I were now in a group of about twelve people - half from our village, the rest from the surrounding area. In fear of being mistaken for an army or rebel militia, we split into smaller groups for the last of the journey. The sun was still shining and two planes were roving around in the sky.

Soon enough, a band of Rhodesian soldiers emerged from the bushes and stopped us; they searched our luggage and asked questions about where we were going and who we had met. All the adults were asked for identification and warned to remember the curfew. They soldiers said that if, after six o'clock, we were found on open ground, we would immediately be shot at. These guys meant business; they had all sorts of guns and grenades, and huge belts of bullets hanging over their shoulders. Unshaven, with heavy packs on their backs, they made an intimidating gang of mostly white mercenaries. They spoke in a funny version of English, so we had to rely on the black soldiers for translation. When we understood, we moved on pretty quickly; there's nothing like a warning of imminent death to make you forget the pain of your blisters. One of our fellow travellers, an old man from my village, had wet his pants out of fear. No one said anything; we simply marched on in silence. When we arrived at the village around six o'clock, all I wanted to do was soak my feet in hot water and sleep. Father had other ideas; after greeting us at the gate of our house, he told me to leave my luggage with mother. I was to follow him. I was to meet the freedom fighters.

Despite the long journey, I was determined to put on a show. I was wearing my red dress, with a blue belt and sandals; I thought I looked very smart and that the girls in the village would be astounded to see how grown up I'd become. As we passed by the local tailor's, a lot of people were moving around very quickly and quietly. Food was being prepared in three-legged chrome pots and plenty of meat had been left on to stew; from the amount of feathers and skin being buried, it looked like at least two goats and several chickens had been slaughtered for the feast. People were sweating from the heat of the fires; either that, or through fear of whatever it was they were obviously on the watch for. A few young men had climbed to the tree-tops and were overlooking every corner of the village. My father wandered around, inspecting everything, then led me behind the tailor's round hut, off towards the little hills nearby. As soon as we reached the bushes, he announced our arrival with slogans of liberation: "Forward with ZANU, Forward with Chimurenga, Viva President Robert Mugabe, Aluta Continua!". This, I soon discovered, was what everyone had to say whenever approaching the freedom fighters' base. As we grew ever closer, my father still repeating the slogans like mantras, we found six men sitting around with a whole bunch of guns and bags brimming with clothes and medical products. Most of the men were wearing jeans or dark clothes; their uniform was effectively menacing, if not quite as professional as that of the Rhodesian Army.

My bright dress suddenly seemed a mistake. Before I had even greeted the men, one of them jumped to his feet, picked up a stick, came over towards me and whacked me hard on the shoulders and twice on my head. It was totally shocking; I wanted to run, but father told me to wait. The man was just about to hit me again when he was held back by one of his colleagues, who told me to go back home and change into something appropriate; the pretty red dress marked me out to the enemy. I did as I was told, quickly heading home and returning to the base in more camouflaged clothes, calling out slogans to announce my arrival.

Despite my initial reception, I soon came to feel at home among the freedom fighters; working for them was exciting, even if, at first, I simply joined the other village girls in cooking and washing their clothes. The comrades moved in groups of twenty-four, though they would often split into smaller bands known as "patios". In each patio, there would be two local boys, called "mujibhas", and three local girls, called "chimbwidos". The mujibhas' job was to patrol their area and watch who was coming and going; it was their responsibility to keep an eye out for enemies and report any suspicious behaviour to their commanders. The chimbwidos cooked, washed and mended clothes, and made sure there were enough blankets for the night - these had to be collected from households in the village and returned to their owners each morning. Villagers would also donate chickens to the cause, and the mujibhas would use their sharp knives for the slaughter. Sometimes, a few goats or a cow would be killed as a bonus; all the animal bones and skin would always be buried so as to help keep the bases a secret. Despite the precautions, many people lost their homes or their lives when they were found to have helped out the comrades; houses would be burnt and innocent people would be shot point blank, or beaten and left to die from their bleeding.

I became a chimbwido; each night, after preparing the freedom fighters' beds, we would walk silently home in the moonlight. This was a short but very risky journey; there was always the chance we'd fall into an ambush and get caught by the enemy. When anyone was caught, and was lucky enough to escape with their life, the freedom fighters would only beat them some more, accusing them harshly of disloyalty and being a mutengesi - a sell-out. Right and wrong were losing their meaning in the heat of the struggle; people would pay for being too clever or being too stupid. "Guerrilla warfare" was the name of the game, and ducking and diving was they only way to survive. A lot of the girls in my village died during this time; some of their bodies have never been found. People grew paranoid; there was no one to trust, and even your parents could become your worst enemies. Walking in the forest, it was impossible to avoid the smell of death or the horrifying sight of rotting corpses, half-eaten by wild animals or half-burnt by the blast of a land mine.

One day, while I was serving lunch to a group of the fighters, I was summoned to another patio, where I found the commander smoking marijuana with other high-ranking officers. I was informed that I'd been nominated to become president of all of the youths in the province. I was to teach and encourage everyone to fully support the struggle. I was to walk with the comrades day and night wherever they went until the war had been won. Until that day arrived, I would no longer be allowed to set foot in the house of my parents; in fact, I was not even allowed to say my goodbyes.

Perhaps the commander expected me to feel pride; all I actually felt, though, was fear. I had already seen the bitterness of the war and witnessed the deaths of so many of the local youths; next time, I felt sure, it would be me who would die. Not that the possibility seemed so terrible; at times, indeed, it felt like the only way out. There was nowhere to run; if I'd tried to escape, the mujibhas would have caught me and killed me without any questions. Sensing my fear, the commander reassured me that, whilst in combat, I would be armed with a sub-machine gun to defend myself and a grenade to use on myself if I was ever surrounded by enemies; being caught alive was never an option - I had too many secrets to spill.

As it turned out, my main duty in the new post was to ensure that the comrades always had enough clothes and shoes, and that the area they were visiting was safe enough to eat, wash and sleep in. I was in the advance party, which meant I was always the first to arrive at an area, do the assessment and send out orders to the chairman of the village. If the camp was new, I would also be required to taste any food and water supplied, checking for poison like a disposable guinea pig. Naturally, this was all terrifying, but I knew that I had no choice. Death was all around, and I couldn't see much difference between bullets or beatings or poison.

Sometimes, I would even have to try on clothes provided by villagers; it wasn't unknown for such gifts to be laced with terrible poisons, causing blindness, or madness, or slow and painful departures. Whenever this happened, the accused would be brutally punished; sometimes, their whole village would pay with their lives. One time, fifteen of my comrades died after putting on poisonous clothes. Somehow, I escaped with my life, but, after an inquiry, my father's name was connected with the delivery of the lethal garments. I was shocked, but refused to believe the terrible rumours; for a start, we were miles away from my village, and there was no reason at all why my father would have been involved in supplying the clothes.

On another occasion, I had gone into a local village to carry out my duties; I was unarmed, as was often the case because everyone now knew who I was; despite my youth, small stature and inability to even handle a gun, I had become respected and somewhat feared throughout the province; enemies even called for the head of Borntosuffernoshungu, the Chimurenga name I'd been given, which translated as "I was born to suffer and I don't care what happens".

I had just been talking to a group of chimbwidos when gunfire cracked out from the roof of the village chairman's house. There were shouts of "chabhenda" - "run for your life" - but, with nowhere to hide, I took the eight girls into the chairman's house and we dived under his big metal bed. We tried to stay silent, but our hearts were beating like mad and our deep breaths were visibly raising the dust from the floor. As my nostrils filled with the stench of blood, I told myself that this was the day; we would be burnt alive in the chairman's house. From outside, we heard screaming voices and the barking of dogs; someone shouted in English for us to come out; not one of us moved. Seconds later, after a deafeningly loud burst of gunfire, my prediction came true: the thatched roof was starting to burn.

I told the girls to get out as soon as they could, holding their hands in the air. When they opened the door, they fell instantly into the arms of our enemies, who wasted no time in kicking and beating them up with their guns. I was terrified but, as the last to come out of the house, I quickly came up with a plan. The leader of the enemy was a big white man with a long red beard and bushy, uncombed hair. As he stood in the dust, wildly swearing, promising death, I walked straight over towards him and started to clap. That got his attention; nearing this horrible beast of a man, I suddenly broke out into some ridiculous dance, miming as though I were deaf and dumb. The soldier paused, looked straight in my eyes, raised his gun, and told me to stop. I didn't. Face to face with this man, and with my own death, I was acting - was I acting? - as though I were now in a trance; moving closer and closer, I reached out and was almost touching his beard. This was life or death; anything could have happened at this precise point.

What happened was this: the solider put down his gun; he laughed, but there was perhaps a touch of fear in his face as he grabbed my hand and led me over to where some of the villagers had been sat in a circle, awaiting their fate. He told them that my parents were to send me somewhere safe; I was clearly unwell and needed protection; it was best to keep people like me away from the dangers of war. Then he turned and walked away, back over to the other girls, who were still screaming with the pain of their beatings. He picked up his gun. He ordered them to shut up and line up; the next sound was the crack of his gun, which was followed by others as the girls were all killed.

I left as soon as the soldiers had gone; I couldn't bear to stay a second with the elders, watching them mourn the loss of their youths, their children.

As they started collecting the bodies, I was head-down, eyes shut, winding my way back to base. I reached home and reported the incident late in the evening; instantly, I was under heavy questioning; it appeared I was right to feel guilty for having survived. Why had all the others been killed, while I had not even been scratched? That much was soon to be changed; I was made to lie down and given a severe beating on my buttocks as a final warning. I was left feeling helpless, so badly bruised that I could no longer feel even pain in my buttocks - they were simply like rocks. That night, we were too scared to stay in the area; it was infested with enemy and we walked through the dark for well over twenty kilometres. There would be no proper food for the next four days; we survived on wild roots, and once killed a jackal, whose heart and liver we devoured uncooked. Some of the freedom fighters even drank its blood; I only feel lucky now that I never saw them drink each other's.

While moving from place to place, we became involved in a lot of combat fighting and many soldiers on both sides died. Sometimes, battles would last from the early hours of the morning to late in the evening; at best, we would emerge blinded by smoke from the gunfire, bombs from the aeroplanes or dust from grenades; at worst, bodies would fly through the air or burn in the napalm. The air was so dirty and hot that we'd constantly suffer from nosebleeds. I was taught to use a sub-machine gun, and hauled my fair share of ammunition; I still had a terrible aim, but being armed made me feel more secure; at least, I now knew I had something to defend myself with if the situation required me to. Far better to die fighting than be shot like a fox, or caught alive and horribly tortured.

It was easiest to catch the mercenaries; those Europeans acted like idiots, inspired by hefty rewards to try and catch freedom fighters in sacks. In combat, they would come straight for us, fighting viciously, but stupidly refusing to give up on their prey. When they themselves were captured, the mercenaries would be tortured with contempt, made to dance and act ridiculously for the entertainment of the villagers before being sentenced to death. Not that it was an easy thing to do, to cheer and laugh at a man you knew was soon to be killed; this was itself another part of the freedom fighters' strategy, an effort to toughen us up and set an example.

With all the moving and fighting, the anger and fear, it was to be eight months before I returned to my village and family. The situation was changing so fast, and so were my duties; on top of my regular tasks, I was now required to sleep with the senior commander; indeed, most of the chibwidos were now falling pregnant. The code of conduct had been broken and the tone of war was darkening. Guerrilla attacks had descended to open warfare; there was no longer a place to call safe. The sky was littered with planes; spotters, Dakotas, jet fighters, helicopters. At times, the sky would blacken with soldiers dropping down in their chutes, meeting a rising hail of bullets from my comrades on the ground. By now, the freedom fighters had anti-air guns, motors, migs, rockets, all sorts of arms from Russia, Yugoslavia, China, Libya, Cuba, Mozambique, Angola, Zambia and all the other countries supporting our struggle. It was in these places that most of our soldiers were trained; their! main base was Maputo, the capital of Mozambique. At one point, I myself almost reached the Mozambique border; in fact, I almost met the whole army's commander, General Josiah Magamba Tongogara. He was a fearsome man, with shoulders like Samson and the face of Chaka the Zulu; his voice boomed and his aura commanded respect. Tongogara was a gallant soldier, and came from the same region as my father, who he knew very well. In the end, we were never to meet; my comrades and I were forced to move base, and headed away from the border. I never met Tongogara and was saddened to hear of his death. To this day, questions are still unanswered about the way that he died.

CHAPTER 9

The war, as you might well have gathered, was now growing extremely bitter indeed. At our bases in Nyadzonya, Tembwe and Chimoi, hundreds of freedom fighters lost their lives to Rhodesian Army bombs. Those who weren't instantly injured or killed were unable to retaliate, caught as they often were in the bath or a state of undress. These mass murders provided the only opportunities for General Petros Wallice, commander of the Rhodesian Army, to claim any kind of success; on the whole, the Rhodesian forces were losing ground, and it was becoming obvious who would win the war. This was the hardest time; people were dying like locusts, soldiers and civilians alike. It was survival of the fittest; our country stank so much of death that even the wild animals and birds had chosen to disappear. In the forests, the only sound was the beating of gunfire, the singing of bombs.

The Rhodesian Army caught me several times. Somehow, I was always set free, and they beatings they gave me were never as harsh as those that I got when I came back to camp. Even at the time, I knew it was amazing I'd survived; someone must surely have been watching over me. The Rhodesian forces knew my father and I by name; we were on their most wanted list. They used to call out our names over loud speakers or drop leaflets listing us alongside other "terrorists" whose capture now warranted rewards. The price on my head was only £10!

For our own safety, my family split up, with relatives changing their names and scattering all over the country. I also took to using false names; this was probably the only reason the Rhodesian soldiers ever let me go. They were pretty stupid, those soldiers. Most of the ones who caught me were European mercenaries who couldn't tell one black person from another. The second time I was caught, they even asked me where Mina and her father were hiding. I told them I had no idea, and that my own name was Debra, which I came up with that second and which has stayed with me since. Amazingly, they believed me.

On one occasion, the mercenaries caught my mother; what's worse, they knew it was her. They asked her where her husband and daughter were. She insisted she didn't know, challenging one of the soldiers to say where his own wife was and whether she knew he was harassing a woman. Angered, the soldiers ordered my mother to start walking away; one of them had his gun aimed at her back. After a couple of steps, she turned round, facing the men squarely, looking them straight in the eyes. They would not shoot her like that; instead, they beat her to within an inch of her life, crushing her ribs with the butts of their guns and leaving her for dead in the backyard of our house. Praise God, she survived, but my mother's ribs and hips were left horribly scarred, and she still suffers pain from that beating today.

As for my father, I used to see him occasionally when he came to visit our bases. He would always tell me he had travelled from far to meet up with a new group of fighters, or that he'd struggled from the city on foot with extra clothes, blankets and medicine. His feet would be covered in blisters, and his beard had become very long. Telling me to take care, he would soon disappear on another of his missions. I thought of my father as fearless, but even he had developed a clear look of worry. No one knew when this war would be over, or who would be left to rebuild.

One day, I was sitting with my comrades in our patio; we had just finished a delicious meal of rice, chicken and vegetables, washed down with cream soda and coke. There had been plenty of meat; it was almost like Christmas had come to the jungle. Everyone was relaxing. The sky was clear and the weather was peaceful, with a fresh breeze rustling through the trees. As often, I was with the commander's group, which included most of our officers. The commander loved to listen to his little radio. At times like this, when it was especially quiet, he would tune in to the afternoon programme, which played lots of local music.

With a loud bang, the party was over. At first, we thought one of our own guns had gone off by mistake, but when the commander tried to get up he lurched violently to the right and his body fell down before me, blood pouring from its chest. He'd been shot. All hell now broke loose; we were surrounded by enemy, there was gunfire all round and people were screaming in panic. Local villagers, who had come to collect our afternoon dishes, were caught up in the confusion and bloodshed. Many of them died, as did a lot of the freedom fighters; we had been totally caught unaware. A fighter plane was dropping bombs; some fell just a few metres from me and I ducked through the bushes to flee them, tearing my flesh on the thorns. I knew I had to fight back - it was my only small chance of escape - but how could I match these trained soldiers; it was difficult enough just to see where to point my gun, let alone pull the trigger!

Looking around me, I saw dead bodies and guns lying all over the floor. I got down on my stomach and crawled across to the weapons. There was an anti-air gun among them; I picked it, found it was already loaded and, realising it was too heavy to carry, decided to use it. I told myself my only hope was to shoot down the plane; whatever happened, I would definitely put up a fight. I aimed; as soon as the fighter plane came into focus, just as it swooped to drop its next load, I fired. I instantly knew that I'd hit it - the tail end of the plane was pouring out smoke - but I didn't hang round to see the results of my shot. It was now time to run for my life. I was holding an unopened grenade, and was ready to throw it or blow up myself. I ran through the jungle, banging into bushes, falling down holes, with bullets hissing past my head. I remembered being once told that if you could hear the sound of the bullet, it had already missed; that gave me the courage to just keep on running. I felt like a charging rhinoceros, possessed with the spirit of my great grandfather's ghost. For miles and miles I ran, aware at each second that my life could immediately end.

Eventually, when my bleeding legs could take me no further, I lay down on the ground, recovered my breath and thought about how to escape. I was away from the worst of the danger, but I knew that running wasn't really the answer; I could easily end up back in the enemy's arms. The sound of their guns was still very clear. The best thing to do was head north; if I turned right at the river, towards the big mountain, I would eventually find my way to a secret cave, which had previously been used by spiritual mediums but had now been taken over by my comrades to hide the wounded and store ammunition. It was a hell of a trek; by the time I arrived, at around six o'clock, I was limping badly, with a horrible thorn in my thigh and heavy belts of bullets and grenades round my neck.

At the mouth of the cave, I announced my arrival by calling out slogans; when the response was positive, I came out from behind a nearby bush and collapsed in exhaustion at one of the freedom fighter's feet. They helped me up, took some of the weapons I was carrying, and were soon pulling out the thorn with a knife. I nearly passed out with the pain, but the freedom fighters praised me for my bravery and said they would send a report to Mozambique on my behalf. We later learnt that the commander hadn't died at the place he was shot; instead, he had tried to crawl and drag his body south, but the Rhodesian forces had followed the trail of his blood. When they caught him, they finished him off, then carried his body to their main training base, where they displayed his corpse as a trophy or warning. In the end, his body was burnt alongside most of the others who died that day. It broke my heart to hear this story; the commander had been a great man. He was a good friend of my father's and had maintained discipline in the freedom fighters' ranks. He had made me feel safe and had never abused me. He was a true soldier and hero; without him, things would undoubtedly change, and probably all for the worse.

My fears were soon confirmed. The freedom fighters quickly grew wild, starting to sleep with young girls, smoke marijuana, and beat people up - sometimes killing them - for little or no reason at all. They became increasingly superstitious, but no amount of voodoo chains or ancestors' spirits could protect them from enemy bullets. With misplaced vengeance, they killed local people for looking like witches, or stammering, or even for being disabled. One old man in my village was murdered for having one testicle bigger than the other. Their favourite targets, though, were prosperous farmers, or church ministers - in fact anyone who had any money. My father protested against these abuses, but the freedom fighters didn't like to be challenged and he was soon listed with other marked men. In the face of so much violence, many people started to suffer horrific hallucinations; it wasn't uncommon to see people running for cover, even when there was no gunfire to be heard or soldiers to be seen. Those who had promised us freedom were now turning against their own people; these were truly disturbing and nerve-wracking times.

Mr Ian Douglas Smith had now joined forces with Bishop Abel Muzorewa, whose army consisted of village boys who had deserted the mujibha ranks. We called these soldiers madzakutsaku: they were a swarm of birds, vainly searching for grasshoppers. With no proper uniform, they patrolled their villages and bases in brown overalls, aimlessly staking out the long-abandoned bases where they themselves had once hidden. Whenever they did chance upon a gang of their former comrades, there would only ever be one winner; the madzakatsaku's light rifles were no match for the freedom fighters' more powerful weapons. They died in large numbers, their bodies being eaten by animals and vultures as no one would give them a burial. Often they fared even worse; the freedom fighters would go straight to the homes of deserters, destroying their houses, stealing their livestock and killing their families. On one occasion, a group of freedom fighters caught about eighty of these local madzakatsaku soldiers. After ordering the boys to stand in a line, the freedom fighters opened fire and murdered them all right in front of the whole village. Those who didn't immediately die were finished off with bayonets. My father had tried to prevent the killings, but met only threats and a warning he was growing too soft. If it really bothered him so much, said one of the freedom fighters, perhaps he would care to join the dead boys.

This was 1979, around the time we first heard that a group of prominent political leaders, including Tongogara and Robert Mugabe, had travelled to England to begin negotiations for peace. They didn't act quickly enough. On

September 9th 1979, my family suffered the most terrible day in its history. At around ten in the morning, I was summoned to the new commander's patio. I arrived to find a group of young boys and girls, all dancing, chanting and taking turns to beat up a naked man who was tied to a post like a chicken. The man whimpered; as I looked up at his face I was horrified to recognise my father.

Shocked, my instant reaction was to turn and run, but one of the freedom fighters caught my arm in his grip and pushed me in front of their prisoner. I stood there, face-to-face with my humiliated father; the man who had made it possible for me to exist was now naked before me, being mercilessly beaten by children. His cries of pain broke my heart. They still do. The beatings didn't stop. I tried to avert my eyes, but the bastards forced up my head and ordered me to join in with the singing and clapping. I couldn't understand; why would these people, these "comrades", who we had served and worked with so long, suddenly turn so horrifically against us. Only later did I learn that the freedom fighters were acting on orders; instructions had come from Mozambique, saying that certain awkward political people were to be eliminated, clearing the way for those who were soon to be coming to power. The future leaders of Zimbabwe wanted no difficult questions asked, and my father was the kind of man who would ask them. He was far from the only one to be killed, though few could have died more horrifically.

The beatings eventually stopped. One of the freedom fighters came to the front, pulled a lighter from out of his pocket and set my fire to my father's beard. Helplessly, I watched on as my father's face burnt. When the fire went out, there was no flesh or hair surrounding his mouth; all you could see were his teeth. A group of freedom fighters pushed him to the ground and started beating his buttocks until they were bleeding. By this point, my father could no longer cry. He was never a prayerful person, my father; he didn't believe in God or Jesus, who he claimed had been made up by white men to brainwash the blacks. But that day he prayed. He asked Jesus to forgive him, and to look after his children and wife. He knew he would never survive; I knew it too. We had seen the freedom fighters in action before, although never this bad.

One of the men turned to me and asked me to bend over and pull down my skirt. I was prepared for a beating; instead, they took turns to sexually abuse me in front of my dying father and all the local boys and girls who were still singing and dancing. I went numb, then fainted from pain. When I came round, the freedom fighters beat me with sticks until my buttocks, too, were heavily bleeding. The men were drinking and smoking marijuana - some were even sniffing white powder. They all looked horrifically pleased with themselves, as tears streamed down the swollen, bloody and blistered face of my father. I still hoped they would let us go; that my father, who was now as good as dead, would at least be able to die in the arms of his wife. Instead, the whole village was ordered to come up to the base; only the sick were excused. In the moonlight - our beatings had lasted all day - a crowd of hundreds assembled. My mother, who had toothache, was thankfully absent from the terrified group, who were ordered to dance and clap to the songs of the war.

In the centre of the gathering, I was forced to sit next to my father, still naked and tied to a pole. One by one, other relatives were thrown in to join us: my younger brother Derrick, who I hadn't seen for weeks, my Uncle Shoko, who was now chairman of the village, and my father's cousin, who, what now seemed like a lifetime ago, had been the first person to tell us about the freedom fighter's struggle. These last two instantly jumped up and started to run; they were caught, tied up and shoved to the floor; bullets were shot through the centre of their skulls.

The freedom fighters turned their guns on my father. Instead of shooting, they stabbed him with their bayonets, piercing his body as if popping a balloon. Blood splattered everywhere, all over me, and when they finally crushed his skull, his body jerked and fell on my lap, his brains scattering all over my legs. As a final act of humiliation, one of the freedom fighters came over and pissed on the corpse of my father.

The three bodies were carried away and destroyed. Rumours said they were buried together in a swamp; a shallow grave with my father in the middle. He was not a perfect man, my father, but he had been tirelessly committed to the cause that had turned so horribly against him. For years, our family had been praying for the end of the war; in an independent Zimbabwe, we told ourselves again and again, our father would find a new freedom, a release from the frustration and anxiety that had plagued him for so long. We were never to witness this change; to this day, no one in my family even knows where my father lies buried. The country we'd fought for had killed him, had murdered my mother's husband. It was heart-breaking beyond belief. There would be no apology, no explanation or compensation – nothing. A dead dog would have been treated with more respect than my father. As for my mother, she was soon the poorest widow in our village. Everyone carried on as though nothing had happened; nobody cared, nobody wanted to know.

Even now, almost thirty years on, the wounds feel fresh. What took place on that day was beyond all description. As I sit at this desk, attempting to map out the horror, I feel it, sharp and undying, in my nerves, my mind and my eyes. It is not something I like to discuss. I never talked of it to my brothers and sisters; they chose to switch off and move on. How could I force them to hear such a horrible truth? How could I wish them to suffer the emotions I'd felt? Perhaps it is a story I should best have taken to the grave; only to help with my healing has it avoided that fate. It is no story. It has wounded me deep. I have built a mask to hide my anguish and pain. In my sleep I grieve to this day.

In the early morning, we were dismissed. I walked home. Around seven, I stood outside my mother's house, covered in blood, my body horrifically swollen. I sat down below our mango tree and gathered the courage to tell my own mother her husband was dead. Her body shook badly. She cried out his name. Sweating, she collapsed on the ground. I knew then the pain would never leave.

The very next day, there arrived an announcement. A ceasefire. The war was over. Innocent people were dead. Millions were heartbroken, homeless or orphaned. Zimbabwe was in turmoil. My father was dead.

Fighting solves nothing. It breeds only terror, revenge and hostility. At its core lies greed, a terrifying hunger for power. In the liberation of our country, had my father been victim or hero? Who can say? All I know is this: his death, in its manner, its timing and its awful incoherence, made a mockery of all of our struggles. His death killed the concept of freedom.

CHAPTER 10

I became very ill. I kept on wetting myself and had terrible stomach pains. I was losing weight, and people in the village were ganging against me, pointing their fingers and blaming me for all kinds of horrible things that had happened. No one seemed to recognise that I myself was a victim of war; that I was a young girl, in need of protection. I felt lost and unwanted. Parents who had lost their own children only seemed to hate me for having survived. My name was dragged through the mud; I was condemned for all kinds of crimes and, though I knew I was innocent, it did no good trying to convince anybody. People were looking for someone to blame, and I was an easy target.

Election campaigns were now up and running, and it was clear that the shift would soon be complete. An amnesty had been agreed; the freedom fighters were invited to temporary camps to register their names and hand over their weapons. A few of Ian Douglas Smith's soldiers were still around to make sure that they did. It was a tricky business; no one really knew what would happen and trust wasn't exactly strong within a temporary government that included such uncomfortable bedfellows as Bishop Abel Muzorewa, Comrade Robert Mugabe, Ian Duncan

Smith and Joshua Nkomo. Some of the freedom fighters chose to stay in the bush; others went straight back home to their families, convinced the new camps were no more than a trick. They stayed vigilant, awaiting instructions and hoarding ammunition.

No one could say for sure that the war was entirely over. Both sides kept men in reserve, ready for signs of a return to the conflict. In the villages, people carried on with the struggle by hiding the fighters and rebuilding their houses and lives. Rhodesian Army soldiers were now patrolling the streets, attacking and intimidating anyone who didn't show support for their party. On one occasion, people were preparing for an opposition rally when the soldiers unexpectedly arrived to disperse them by randomly firing their weapons. When news spread of this story, one of the villagers cooked up a rumour that it was me who had grassed up to the soldiers. The freedom fighters didn't bother with questions; coming straight to my mother's house, they found me asleep on the veranda and started to beat me up. I was only saved by the honesty and courage of one local teacher, who insisted I wasn't to blame. I had been sleeping for hours; I was sick, hadn't heard of the rally or seen! any soldiers for days. I was deeply hurt and disturbed that people could treat me so bad. Their beating definitely didn't help my recovery.

In the end, mother had to take me for treatment at Chiredzi Hospital, where my brother was now working as an administrator. Uncle Peters was still running his business, fixing radios in the local township. The journey was far from easy; there were still problems with transport as a result of the landmines and my legs were both horribly swollen. At one point, we caught a ride in a scotch-cart pulled by two starving donkeys. They took us ten miles; we walked for three hours before finding more transport. My bare feet cracked and burnt in the heat. All in all, it took us two and half days to reach our destination. I arrived exhausted, filthy and hungry, in a great deal of pain.

After stopping in at Uncle Peters' shop, where we refuelled with soft drinks and buns, we went straight to my brother's house. My sister was there, preparing the lunch, and the smell of good food was all it took to revive us. We ate, washed our clothes and enjoyed our first showers in days before heading back to Peters' house, where my grandmother met us with tears in her eyes. That evening, we all sat out on the veranda as mother told tales of the war and spoke of the death of my father. I didn't say much.

In the years since we'd seen her, my sister had grown very large. She was now dating a man who worked at Bata Shoe Shop as a salesman. She seemed happy and so much in love; in fact, she spent most of the evening telling me how wonderful he was. I wanted to show her I cared, but my mind kept on drifting away. My ears buzzed; I could have sworn I smelt blood in the air. The next day, I was taken to hospital, where I was admitted immediately and ended up staying for weeks. The doctors said I was underweight and suffering from all sorts of infections. By the time I was well enough to leave, mother had already headed home to take part in the elections. Without her, I spent much of my time with my sister, visiting the local town centre to meet up with her man. We took in a lot of the local sights, sometimes going to Triangle Sugar Plant or down to Chiredzi River or even for weekends at Tambuta Hotel Lodge. On Sundays, we would go to church, then on to the football stadium to watch the afternoon game. I loved it when my brother was playing; he was never professional, but to me he was always the star.

I put on weight, growing into a rounded young lady with nicely smooth skin. For a while, I was happy; all seemed well and my brother had even agreed I should go back to school. I had been in Chiredzi for roughly six months, and life had been growing surprisingly sweet, when I was devastated by the news that I had to return to the village. Mother needed help with tilling the land and all of her endless chores. I didn't want to go back to a place of such horrible memories. As always, though, I had no choice; even my sister was set to come too, although she'd secretly said she was pregnant and had no intention of staying there long.

Back in the village, things had changed for the worse. People had switched off and there was a general air of unfriendliness. I was lonely, and desperately thankful to be with my sister until she headed off back to her man. Mother had decided that all the family were to go back to school. I was to repeat my last year, which made me uncomfortable; most of my class-mates would be much younger than me. A few other girls repeated too, but most of them never finished the year because they got pregnant by either their teachers or men in the village. At one point, even I was infatuated with one of my teachers, though I quickly turned off when I discovered he'd been sleeping with one of the local girls who everyone said had gone mad.

School was full of war stories. At night, I used to have nightmares about my father's death. Something had to change if I was ever going to be able to move on with my life. With Zimbabwe now an independent nation, I decided there was no reason to suffer in silence; I would simply meet the new President and find out where my father was buried. Perhaps, I could even get some form of compensation for my mother, who was now struggling to feed, clothe and educate her children. My brother wasn't helping much; he had married and started a family, which he could barely support off his own little salary. Villagers noted how my mother could barely manage to till all her fields; instead of helping, they started bullying her and stealing her land. We had no oxen to plough our fields, so mother had to wait for the others to finish before begging to borrow their animals. Thankfully, God was always gracious to us; despite being the last ones to plough, we would always harvest enough to keep us fairly well-fed, with a little extra to sell to the Grain Marketing Board. We were lucky that mother's fields were so fertile, and the rain always seemed to come just in time for our crops. Unsurprisingly, our good fortune made the other farmers jealous. The way they tried to make mother's life difficult was what drove me to seek out a portion of justice. Mother had fought hard in the struggle for freedom; she didn't deserve to keep suffering now. Sometimes, I would h! ear her in the early hours of the morning as she cried out to God and mourned the terrible loss of her husband. Her tears broke my heart. I became determined to do something to make her life better. Piece by piece, I came up with a plan.

One evening, just after supper, I approached mother and told her I needed ten dollars for a trip that had been arranged by my school. This was the first time that I'd ever asked her for money, so she trusted my words and gave me the dollars without any questions. I was lucky in another way, too, because earlier that afternoon the Christian Care Organisation had visited our house, leaving thirty dollars behind to help out the family. Although I felt bad taking the money in such a deceitful manner, I told myself that, once I had succeeded in my plans, I would pay mother back and apologise for lying. The next morning, I left the house early. I didn't want mother to quiz any of my class-mates about this sudden school trip.

When the school bells were ringing, I was already a few miles down the road, about to board the early bus to Gweru. I was still in school uniform, so I only had to pay half fare: two dollars fifty. The bus reached Gweru at about ten o'clock, and I jumped straight on the next one to Harare, the newly named capital of Zimbabwe. The ticket cost six dollars fifty, so I was now left with less than two dollars. On the journey, I picked up an old newspaper with names and pictures of the new cabinet members. It was the President I wanted to see; I was determined to talk to him face-to-face. I wanted to tell him the story of my father, of a man who had fought for his country, was betrayed by his comrades, and had disappeared from the face of the earth. I needed to know where his body was buried; if we could find him, and move him, and re-bury him close, only then would we find any peace.

I wasn't entirely naive. I was old enough to know that you couldn't just turn up and walk straight into the President's office. I decided to pay my first visit to the Deputy Minister of Home Affairs, who was my local MP and originally came from my village. On the bus, between naps, I had planned out my tactics and speech. Many people were afraid of the new government figures; it was claimed they were as fierce as freedom fighters during the war. They wore dark suits, and travelled with armed guards in blacked-out Mercedes. Whenever they passed by, people would stand still and salute. Other cars would move out of their way.

I was nervous, but there was no turning back. I had never been to Harare, and had little idea what would happen or where I would stay for the night. People moved fast in the city. Even the beggars seemed busy as they asked for loose change from the well-dressed people passing by on the streets.

CHAPTER 11

Upon reaching the main bus terminal, I was immediately overwhelmed by the noise and chaos. People were selling food, newspapers, all manner of goods; others were scrambling onto buses as they pulled out the station; still more were just hanging around, looking for all the world as though they were waiting to steal the next sucker's wallet.

This was Mbare Market, home to the famous Matapi flats and Machipisa, the biggest supermarket I'd ever seen in my life. Mbare was a black working-class district, notorious for thieves, fighters, hookers and witch doctors. I'd heard tales of it all of my life; now I was finally here, feeling dizzy, lost and confused. I asked the conductor where I could catch a bus further into the city. He pointed off towards a long unruly queue of people; shouting and swearing, they appeared to be doing all that they could to raise up a big cloud of dust. How would I ever get to the front of *that*? Luckily, I had size on my side. When the bus quickly arrived, and everyone surged for the door, I was able to squeeze on while others were still left outside, cursing their luck in the heat. Not that I survived unscathed; someone had stepped on my bare foot and crushed my big toe, which was still painful from when I'd recently banged into a rock while running to arrive at school on time! . My toe was now bleeding, the nail hanging loose, but nobody noticed my pain. At least I'd fared better than a boy who'd tried to climb in through one of the windows; the angry crowd had pulled him back, tugging down his trousers as he tumbled in onto the seats. Everyone noticed him, alright!

I paid half fare - fifty cents - and asked the driver to let me know when we'd reached the government buildings. He did, and I alighted. Someone else pointed me in the direction of Samora Michael Way, named after the late president of Mozambique, who had been a great supporter of the struggle in Zimbabwe. Samora Michael had a beautiful wife called Graca; you might well know this, but Graca was later to marry Mr Nelson Mandela when he finally divorced from his first wife, Winnie.

Anyway, I'd now finally reached my destination: the Ministry of Home Affairs. Its building was also home to the High Court of Zimbabwe, and I felt my stomach turn cold with fear as I climbed three flights of stairs before gold letters on a door announced my arrival. A big desk was directly in front of me, and a few well-dressed people were sitting in comfortable chairs on one side of it. I quickly understood it was some kind of counter; behind the desk sat a lady, roughly my mother's age, who seemed very polite and approachable. She looked at me with sympathy through her big wide glasses, and asked in a soft voice how she could help. She had the air of a dormitory mistress from some old-fashioned boarding school, but there was also a touch of bemusement in her expression; I must have looked very odd in that room, a small shabbily dressed girl among all the smart adults.

Plucking up courage, I told her I had come all the way from my village and wanted to see the Deputy Minister of Home Affairs. I even told her why. She listened in silence, scribing my words in what appeared to be hieroglyphics, before telling me to wait in an empty chairs while she asked the Minister whether he would have time to see me or not. She disappeared through the huge glass doors, returning after a few minutes with the news that, yes, the Minister would see me, but that I would have to wait to the very end of the day - I was to be the very last person he saw. That didn't matter to me; I thanked the lady politely and sat comfortably back in the chair, watching the office proceedings, the various visitors and the lady herself as she juggled several telephone receivers and attended to all the enquiries. Boy, did that lady smell good! Every few minutes, a whiff of her perfume would fill the whole room. She kept on glancing up at me; sometimes our eyes would meet an! d she'd smile. At one point, she got up from her desk and brought me over a sandwich and a soft drink, which I more than happily accepted. I thanked her once again for her kindness.

After what seemed like hours, a beautiful lady pushed through the big glass doors and wandered straight over towards me. She was very expensively dressed, with her hair done up like a cake, and her tights and stilettos perfectly complimenting her elegant legs. She appeared to be walking on air - if I'd met her by a river, I would have sworn she was some kind of mermaid! The lady gave me her name and told me she was secretary to the Minister. The lady at the desk offered me a very reassuring wink as the secretary started to ask me some questions, noting my answers in a small blue pad. She then led me through the glass doors, along a small passageway with a bright red carpet and through an oak double door into a beautiful office with a desk full of telephones and a huge typewriter right at its centre. The room was full of fresh flowers and plants, which must have been well taken care of because they were shining with bright green life. Here, I was asked to wait while the secretary knocked on a brown door in the corner and quickly disappeared inside. I was nervous and hungry; my stomach was growling. When the secretary soon reappeared, she held the door open and summoned me in to the Minister's room. I entered slowly, shutting the door behind me.

I stood face to face with the Minister. Walking round his spectacular desk, he gestured for me to sit in a leather chair that looked as though it had probably never been sat in before. Boy, was it comfortable! He sat down on another chair facing me. We greeted each other. Hesitantly, I introduced myself and told him my story. The more I spoke about my family, the more confident I became, until I was almost possessed, pouring out things I'd never thought I could ever have said. By the time I had finished, tears were running down my cheeks and the Minister's face was full of pity. He picked up a telephone from the table near his chair and started telling someone about all the things that I'd said. When he hung up, he reminded me that he was not only the Deputy Minister for Home Affairs, but was also my Member of Parliament; I had definitely come to the right office. He assured me that he knew my father, and that the government was well aware of his great contribution to t! he struggle for independence. I felt at peace; they knew my father after all!

At this point, the Minister looked down at my feet and noticed they were bare and that my big toe had started bleeding again. He asked if it was hurting; I nodded my head. He stood up and went into the next room - his bathroom - returning with a first aid kit, from which he took out a plaster and proceeded to cover the wound. He then asked me where I was planning to spend the night; I told him at the bus terminal next to the market. I also told him that I didn't have money for the return fare home. Telling me not to worry, he picked up the phone and was soon gently explaining to someone that he would be bringing a visitor home - "the daughter of an old political friend from my constituency". What a man this Minister was; within minutes, he was not only inviting me to stay at his house, but was practically begging me to fetch mother and come and live as a part of his family! He even said he would arrange for me to go back to school.

But first things first; the Minister still had a few things to clear up in his office, so I went back to the secretary's room to wait for him to finish. The secretary herself had now left, and the whole place had fallen silent and eerie. Two men came in, greeted me politely, and knocked at the Minister's door. When he emerged, holding a briefcase, the two men - who I soon realised were his driver and bodyguard - instantly saluted and led us out of the office in silence. I was gripped by excitement and wild curiosity. Riding in the back of a brand-new Mercedes with a government minister; for the first time in my life, I felt truly important! In a cream leather seat, I stretched out my legs and breathed in the aroma of the luxurious car and the Minister's beautiful after-shave.

The Minister lived in the Highlands area, where all the houses were surrounded by walls that made it almost impossible to see into their gardens. As we arrived at his big iron gates, a policeman with a rifle opened them for us, then stood violently still and saluted. We drove into an open garage near a big white house facing a beautiful swimming pool. The garden had all sorts of flowers and plants, and everything looked in perfect condition. The car doors were opened for us, and the Minister asked me to follow him into the house. His wife and two youngest children came out to greet him, though none seemed to notice my presence. The Minister's wife was mixed race, with strong European features that had passed down to her children. Eventually, she told me to go downstairs to join the other children, who were apparently watching TV.

I walked along a huge corridor, its floor full of well-polished tiles, then down the stairs to a room in which four children were sitting on sofas. I say children, but the two boys must have been roughly eighteen; the girls were slightly older than me. The Minister, who had followed me down, quickly introduced me to his family; the two boys and one of the girls were his children; the other girl, in glasses, was his sister. I greeted them politely and they warmly responded, asking me to join them on the sofa to watch television. The Minister left, one the boys switched the TV back on, and we all proceeded to watch what I soon realised was their favourite soap, "Dallas". The kids seemed to know all the characters; even I, watching for the very first time, was quickly caught up by the escapades of those beautiful ladies and their rich gentleman, "JR". I was also struck by how the house in Dallas looked a lot like the Minister! e s home; I was among the rich and famous, a long way from my mother's crumbling hut, with its worn thatched roof that leaked in the rain. I thought of how, when the storms were especially strong, that roof would leak so much that the rain would put out our fire; all we could do was cuddle up beside the wooden door and sing songs from the Methodist Hymn book. Our favourite was called "Jerusalem, my happy home". In the Minister's house, I felt like I'd finally entered that happy home. This was a house fit for God; a house full of lights and warmth, where everyone was educated, and spoke only in English, and smelt really good. I felt like a fish out of water. My mind started swimming in circles and the evening seemed to go on forever.

I quickly learnt the way things worked in the household. Everyone was related, but the Minister, his wife and their two youngest children led an almost separate life to the others. They dined apart, eating different food, and their bedrooms, with en-suite bathrooms, were located on the first floor of the house. I was to sleep upstairs with the two other girls, sharing a toilet and shower. The older boys slept next door in a cottage. My bedroom had a lovely bed with clean sheets and covers, but I instantly decided not to sleep in it. There was no way I was going to wet that bed, or stain it with blood from my toe. As soon as I was on my own, I locked the door, took one of the pillows from the bed and lay down on the carpeted floor. That was definitely comfortable enough for me; I was used to sleeping on hard surfaces and, anyway, I was far too tired to have any trouble getting to sleep.

The next morning, I was woken by the sound of a gentle knock on the door; when I opened it, one of the girls handed me a towel and a beautiful flowery dress, with a pair of knickers and some smart blue sandals. I went into the bathroom, took a lovely warm shower and changed into the nice new clothes. The dirty ones I wrapped up inside a plastic bag, then I waltzed out of the bedroom and down the stairs to join the others for breakfast. Everyone greeted my appearance with approval, and the Minister told me to hurry because he was taking me back to his office. On the way, he asked me how I'd slept, to which I politely replied that I'd slept very well and that his house was very beautiful and that I was very grateful for all his support and exceptional hospitality. He pointed out some of the most interesting landmarks and we chatted our way to the office.

At the Ministry of Home Affairs, the receptionist was already busy with her never-ending calls. She clearly approved of my new outfit, too, and welcomed me back with a very friendly hello. The Minister headed straight to his office while his secretary made me a nice cup of tea and buttered scone. When he called me in, I found him waiting on one of the big leather chairs, a small bundle of money on the table beside him. Counting the notes, he handed me five hundred dollars, saying it was to pay for my journey back home and my return the next Monday with mother. Anything that was left should be used to buy food on the way and a few groceries to take back to my family.

My heart skipped and my hands started shaking; I'd never handled so much money in my life. The Minister reassured me that he would put the notes in an envelope and in a small handbag; he seemed almost pleased by my obvious nerves, and quickly informed me that his driver and bodyguard were waiting downstairs to drive me back down to the terminal. He shook my hand, and told me again to come back the following Monday. Today was Friday. As I left the Minister's office, I thanked his beautiful secretary and said goodbye to the lovely receptionist. From her desk, she pulled out a shiny black book, which she handed to me as a present. When I saw that it was a leather-bound bible, tears welled up in my eyes and I thanked her for the kind generosity. I could see that she was almost crying, too, but that the tears were hidden behind her big round glasses and unflappable air of professionalism.

Clutching the bible, I emerged from the Minister's office. There was money in my bag and the mission had been a success. I felt like a hero! The city itself was packed full of shoppers. Speeding cars raced down the streets, and the sound of police sirens seemed to come from all over. Either they were busy catching criminals or simply chaperoning the president's motorcade through the streets of Harare - who knew! I suddenly wondered why everyone had got to know me so quickly, why they had just automatically accepted me as one of them. Things had worked out so perfectly that I felt like a fairy princess. In the big black Mercedes, I was beginning the long journey home, where I would undoubtedly have a lot of explaining to do. Would mother believe me? Would she agree to come back to Harare? I suddenly panicked; what if she refused? Would I be arrested for wasting the Minister's time and stealing his money?

The bus terminal was just as noisy as the day before - had it only been the day before! Men were busy loading luggage on roofs and passengers were rushing to buy some last-minute items and wave all their relatives goodbye. I was dropped off right in front of my bus; everyone stared to see who would get out of the big black Mercedes. The

Minister's bodyguard escorted me to the bus and told the conductor to look after me well. I was put in a seat that was next to the driver, facing all the other passengers. It was a very privileged position that said I was someone important. When the conductor gave me my ticket, he also asked me to write a list of the groceries that I wanted to buy for my mother. I quickly jotted down bread and butter, and my mother's favourite marmalade jam. The conductor gave the list to one of the men who was loading the luggage; within a few minutes, the man had rushed off and returned with a mountain of groceries - a whole wheel-barrow full! ! There was bread and butter, and marmalade jam, and sweets and biscuits, and half a leg of beef. I wasn't asked to pay for anything; the conductor said it had all been taken care of. Even my bus fare had been already paid for.

We departed around ten, heading straight for the busy motorway that passed through Chegutu, Kadoma, Kwe-Kwe and Gweru before finally arriving in Bulawayo. We would turn off just after Gweru, driving through Shurugwi, my nearest big town, then Cha-Cha-Cha, Hange, Mbiri, Dombwe and then reach my village, Ziyambi. From chatting to a few local people, I soon realised why the conductor had been so amazingly kind - the Minister actually owned the bus I was travelling in, as well as a number of businesses, including supermarkets in Harare, farms in Chegutu and houses all over the country. When we arrived in my village, the bus pulled up right outside my mother's gate and the conductor carried the groceries into her yard. Mother was holding a hoe, and had clearly just come back from the fields. The driver added to her confusion by saying he would pick us up on Monday morning at nine o'clock sharp. I would explain all the rest, he said with a smile.

As the bus drove away, mother demanded to know where I had been, why I had lied, and where I had got all that shopping. She had so many questions that I couldn't work out which one to answer first, so I started by simply apologising, then proceeded to tell her the whole crazy story. Soon she was crying and my brothers and sisters were looking on in amazement, largely focused on the big heap of unopened goodies. The aroma of fresh bread was so strong and tempting that cockroaches started falling from the roof of the house. I took the envelope out of my handbag and handed it over to mother; upon opening it, she almost fell over. Inside, along with the money, was a letter from the Minister that backed up my story. If I'd known it existed, I could have saved all my breath. As it was, I was glad that I'd told the whole story; I wanted mother to hear every detail, not just the words in the letter.

We ate a hefty dinner and packed all the groceries safely away, then my brother was sent to fetch my aunt and one of her church colleagues, who was married to the village chairman. Word had apparently spread through the village that I had eloped with a mystery man, so the new visitors were somewhat surprised to see me back home, relaxing on the veranda as mother prepared afternoon tea with bread and butter and marmalade. My aunt and the chairman's wife quickly persuaded mother to go with me on Monday morning to Harare as requested in the letter. We said some prayers, and the visitors left with their own little share of the groceries. Mother was always a generous lady; she gave the best of what she had, not simply the things that she no longer wanted. She gave, but rarely received; in a strange way, she proved the truth of that old adage, "it is easier to give than receive".

The rest of the weekend flew by in a haze of preparation for the big journey to Harare. I was so excited, desperately looking forward to our new life in that big white house as part of the Minister's family. By the time we left for Harare, the whole village knew nearly everything; my aunt was far from shy in spreading the story, and took considerable pleasure in visiting others and swapping her gossip for treats. She was particularly fond of a good cup of tea with plenty of milk and, boy, didn't everyone know it!

When we got to the bus stop that morning it was as if the whole of the village had come out to wave us goodbye. A group of old women started to sing hymns, and danced with surprising agility the second they caught sight of the bus. I felt like royalty, though it was clear that an undercurrent of natural jealousy had infected large parts of the crowd. The best seats on the bus had already been reserved for us. The vehicle was full, with some people standing, but two big seats had been kept specifically for mother and I. The conductor, who was obviously angling for promotion, made sure we were well-fed and looked-after all of the way to Harare. He kept reminding me to mention his name to the Minister and tell him how kind he had been.

When we arrived at Mbare Market, the Minister's driver and bodyguard were already waiting to give us a lift in the big black Mercedes Benz. They took us straight to the Minister's office, where I was happy to see that the nice lady was still sat behind her big desk. I introduced her to my mother, and they spoke for a few minutes. Mother thanked her for her kindness, and the lady told her how lucky she was to have such a brave daughter as me. I gave her a smile and she flashed me another one of her winks. They were magic, those winks; they could have melted even the hardest of hearts.

Mother and the lady were just realising something they had in common - they were both preachers in the Methodist Church - when the

Minister's secretary came into the room, greeted my mother and invited us into the Minister's office, where tea and biscuits were waiting for us on the coffee table right next to the big leather chairs. Mother greeted the Minister in very polite terms, using his totem in some poetic way that I had never encountered before. The Minister was obviously impressed; his face lit up with a smile and we launched into a long conversation, punctuated by biscuits and dominated largely by mother.

After tea, the Minister got up and went to his desk to make a few phone calls. He came back with the exciting and unexpected news that the Vice-President was now ready to meet us. Seeing our obvious anxiety, the Minister reassured us that he would be there to support us so there was no need to feel worried. The Vice-President's office was just across the main road in Samora Michael Avenue, but we apparently still needed a couple of bodyguards to escort us. When we got there, I was struck by how grand and shiny everything looked. A lot of big men in dark suits were standing round the reception, with guns and walkie-talkies hanging off their belts. On seeing the Minister, they all saluted, directing us straight into the Vice-President's office without any questions.

We passed along a very long corridor with a red carpet and a lot of oak double doors, each with its own security keypad, which our guide decoded with ease. In the Vice-President's office itself, there were another eight big men waiting for us. They were all sat round in big armchairs, surrounded by a huge table that could probably have accommodated half of my village. The table, like everything else, was extremely well-polished; I could see my reflection in it as easily as looking in the mirror. As we entered, everyone in the room immediately stood up, except, of course, for the Vice-President, who remained in his big leather chair. After a period of greetings and introductions, the room fell silent. The Vice-President picked himself out of his chair and came over to personally greet my mother. Looking at her straight in the face, he burst into loud, infectious laughter; it turned out he had recognised her from the detention centre in Gonakudzingwa where he had earlier been detained with my father. In fact, before he had been sent to the centre, the Vice-President had regularly hidden in my mother's granary; every day, she used to bring him some food and a bucket to use as a toilet. What a crazy coincidence! On top of that, we soon worked out that the Vice-President was actually vaguely related to my mother; some member of his family shared the same totem as her.

The Vice-President never went to school; most of his education had taken place in the in Gonakudzingwa. Although he had only completed standard six, he was a clearly intelligent man, dignified and respected by most for his lack of corruption. He offered my mother the platform to speak. She was a good speaker, mother; in fact, an excellent public speaker. She really knew how to reach to the core of her audience's hearts. It was for that reason that she became such an outstanding preacher for the Methodist church. Yet I was still surprised and uplifted to watch her confidently address these highly respected men in their dark pin-striped suits. They all drowned in her speech, those men, nodding their heads, some even sweating a little, maybe through guilt. My mother would use certain words and phrases to explain a situation so that even the dullest person could easily understand. Her words of wisdom still ring in my ears whenever I am faced by a difficult challenge.

When she had finished her speech, the room was filled with a deep silence that confirmed she had made her point well. The men in the room seemed to look smaller than before, and some were wiping sweat from their foreheads. One by one, each of them spoke; though none of them supplied the apology I'd been waiting to hear, they did promise my mother she would be well looked after, that all of her children would be sent back to school and that the Government would build her a comfortable new home and also replace all her livestock. She was now an official State Widow, which meant that the Government would make sure she got practically everything she could want, including state compensation for my father's death that amounted to something in the region of fifty thousand dollars a year for life. The first instalment would be paid the very next month, along with a further fifty thousand dollars to cover the costs of rebuilding our home. It was also agreed that the Government would properly investigate the death of my father and make sure that he received an appropriate burial. As for me, the Minister told the group that he had decided to take me as a part of his family; whatever money was expected to be paid for my education should be passed on directly to him. Everything had worked out so well; mother had been treated with the utmost respect and I had achieved something great for my family and could look forward to an exciting new life in the city.

After the meeting, the Minister took us both back to his house and made arrangements for mother to stay for another day before heading home to the village. She left the next morning, stocked up on goodies and with the Government promises still ringing in her ears. I stayed behind, ready to start my new life in the Minister's house, living like one of his children. It seemed like our struggle was over.

Yet, of all the promises made on that day in the Vice President's office, none were to become a reality. Right up to this day, not a single penny has been paid to my mother. And worse was to come.

CHAPTER 12

It took little more than a week for the Minister to find me a place to study - and, boy, what a place it was! I was due to enrol as a pupil at Species College in Rhodes Avenue, which was one of the most expensive schools in the whole of Zimbabwe. I found it slightly strange that the street was still named after Cecil John Rhodes, a man who had apparently discovered Rhodesia - along with all of the Africans who'd already been living there for thousands of years!

Anyhow, my chosen subjects were English History, Geography, Bible Knowledge and Home Economics, all to be studied at O Level, now known as GCSE. I was also required to do a skill-based course that would to allow me to find employment easily after my studies were done. I chose Shorthand, Typing and Reception.

The College was still full of white tutors, who were experiencing obvious difficulties with the number of black faces that had infiltrated their ivory towers. I distinctly remember one occasion when we were in class and one of the teachers came in and asked for all of the black girls to come to the toilets. Once we were gathered in the WC, she proceeded to demonstrate how to use the equipment properly! I felt extremely insulted and didn't hesitate to report the teacher to the Minister, who responded by ensuring that she was quickly suspended from Species. The next thing I heard, she had apparently emigrated to South Africa, which was pretty much the normal thing that most white people did whenever they met strong opposition or felt that black people had invaded their space.

I did learn some new tricks from my white teachers, though. Once, one of our teachers asked all the black students to hold out their hands. She then came down the line, examining our pitiful nails; some were extremely dirty or broken, others had horrible scratches all over their surface. The teacher insisted we file them; having no idea what a nail file was, I spent the whole afternoon trudging round city bookshops looking for what I thought would be some kind of folder, perhaps where you should store all your nails whenever you cut them. Who was I to know that a nail file was some kind of long stick with rough flat sides?

On the whole, college was fun, and, as the Minister's "daughter", I was treated with much more respect than I had been before. I liked my typing lessons; we learnt how to touch type, practising with strange stock phrases like "the quick brown fox jumped over the lazy dog", or, the one I liked most, "this is the time for all good men to come to the aid of the party!". These sentences sounded oddly romantic to me; I would type them so fast that I always came out with good grades. Very quickly, I had progressed from thirty five words a minute to sometimes over eighty. It was fantastic! I also made a few good friends, or perhaps not so much friends as hangers-on - people who liked the idea of being close to the Minister's daughter. They often used me as a cover that allowed them to get away with all kinds of naughty activities, such as once, when we went to a coffee shop and none of us had enough money to pay; the other girls introduced me to the cafe manager, who was well aware of the Minister's power. We didn't pay for our coffee and scones that day, and no one ever made a fuss.

I soon had a few admirers, too; bank managers, company directors, lecturers from the famous University of Harare. They would take my friends and I out for lunch, but always backed off once they realised my connection to the Minister. I'd never felt so secure and protected; nothing was going to get in the way of my plans for the future! Each morning, I would join the Minister in his big black Mercedes as he drove into work. I used to hang around the reception, sometimes enjoying a cup of tea with the lovely lady at the big desk. Then the Minister's secretary would bring some loose change for my lunch and I'd start the twenty-minute walk down a few blocks past the big

Methodist Headquarters Church to Species College.

In the evenings, after college, I would walk back to the Minister's office and wait for a lift with him home. As soon as we arrived, I would join the others in the kitchen to prepare for our supper. The Minister's wife worked as a partner at a firm of solicitors; at a later stage, she opened her own firm with the help of the Minister, who also used to juggle his government duties with occasional work as an advocate. He was very good at the job, and I'm sure that he loved it; people used to travel from far and wide for his advice and representation. Of course, working in the Home Office and being friends with the Attorney General gave the Minister a certain advantage, but both he and his wife had been highly trained at one of the leading universities in England.

In order to ensure that his office ran smoothly, the Minister's wife would generally be the one who represented their clients in court; they definitely had a strong partnership that went way beyond marriage, which was just as well, as the Minister had a tendency to play away from home. By the time he died tragically in a car accident, the Minister had become father to countless children from all kinds of women; for him, choosing a woman was simply a matter of searching for skirts. The man was simply addicted to sex, and that was the bottom line! He'd met his wife at the Africa

Centre in King's Street, London, when they were both students. It was a place where all educated Zimbabweans and prominent political members used to hang out, and where many white women would go looking for black men. There was, so it seemed, a lot of love and lust at the Africa Centre; many marriages were known to have begun there.

The Minister's wife would always be home by the time we got back, busy preparing a special supper for her husband and children in the same kitchen that we also used. The Minister seemed to have little control over the division within his own family; he was simply caught in the middle and, though I'm sure he would have preferred for us all to eat together, he chose to ignore the problem for the sake of his wife. We didn't find it difficult, either; it gave us independence to cook and eat whatever we liked, without any restrictions; sometimes, the Minister would even pop in and ask us to spare him some sadza. Boy, did he love sadza, especially with the sour milk that he brought from his farm every weekend.

When the school reports were published, I would always rush home to show the Minister and his wife; it made me feel so happy to hear them praising my efforts and encouraging me to work even harder. I was proud of my achievements, and could now manage a good conversation in English, without stammering or feeling shy with my grammar. I had always told myself that one day I was going to speak English; that dream was finally coming true.

One weekend, the Minister suggested that I join him at the farm to help out, since there wasn't much work to be done in the big white house. Only the elder boys and "Auntie" - the Minister's sister - were allowed out at weekends; the rest of us spent Saturdays at the local Seventh Day Adventist Church and had our own little rituals for Sundays, when we did the laundry, prepared for school, and watched heaps and heaps of television. I was particularly fond of "Dallas", "Dynasty", "Fame", and "Mind Your Language". On Thursdays, we would all gather round the TV for an hour of local music followed by the drama of "Mr Mukadota", which was like a Zimbabwean version of "East-Enders". It was extremely interesting - the pick of the week!

Anyway, I agreed to go to the farm, feeling that it was a good way of showing my gratitude for all that the Minister had done. From then on, we would rush home on Friday evenings, I would quickly pack my weekend clothes and, after supper, we'd drive off in one of the family cars - a Peugeot 505 as far as I can recall. On the journey, the Minster would ask me all kinds of questions about my studies and how I was finding life in his household. He then used to tell me all sorts of stories about his work in the Government, and sometimes more personal things about himself and his family, like how he married his wife, little things about his children, his parents' relationship, and so on. He told me jokes that were occasionally embarrassing; those ones he would laugh at the most! It seemed almost as though I had become his personal confidant. I got insider gossip on all of the Government figures, including the President; the Minister seemed to think many of his colleagues were simply a waste of space. All the while, he would be driving the car at incredible speeds and I would be holding my breath, gasping whenever we came close to hitting a rabbit or hedgehog - and we must have hit our fair share!

At the farm itself, I worked hard with the labourers, helped the Minister to count out his money from the weekly sales, and then headed off to the nicely thatched weekend house to prepare dinner for the Minister and myself. I made the food so well that the Minister would always finish everything on his plate, almost to the point of licking it clean. Boy, did he love my cooking! After dinner, I get his bed ready, ran him a nice warm bath, then retired to my room and switched on my favourite shows. I did all this with such simple innocence because it was basically the same as I'd been doing for most of my life as a servant. It was only natural for me to do all the chores without being told; I was already a responsible young woman, and had been for years. To be honest, I was happy to help out the Minister; he was almost like my own father, and I was simply repaying his kindness. For his part, the Minister seemed happy to have me around, and soon suggested that I join him every week! end out at the farm; it would make his workload a lot easier and my company and cooking would make his life brighter. Not for one moment did it even cross my mind that his intentions might not all be so pure.

On school holidays, I was always allowed to visit my mother back home in the village. I would take a lot of meat from the farm, along with eggs, rice, cans of sour milk and a whole heap of goodies from the Minister's supermarket, as well as some cash for my mother. Everything would be loaded on the bus, which took me straight to my family's front gate. My younger brothers and sisters would always be waiting in excitement, but it grew increasingly clear that others in the village were far from happy to see me. Jealousy had spread and many of the villagers hated that we were enjoying these privileges. Some even went as far as Harare to protest to the Minister himself, telling him lies about my role in the war and saying how sorry he would be one day when he realised I couldn't be trusted. One day, after college, I even bumped into our village chairman coming out of the Minister's office; apparently, he had come to warn the Minister about me and offer one of his own innocent daughters instead. It was sickening to hear all the horrible stories being made up against me. It made me sad to think that people could hate you for just being smart. The Minister would always explain everything to mother and me, and we grew used to brushing it all off as nothing. Mother would never asked anyone why they had been spreading these rumours about her own daughter; she simply believed that the truth would prevail, and was never a woman who sought confrontation.

One holiday, things turned particularly nasty. I was at my mother's home as usual; she was heading off to one of her regular church meetings and my sister and I decided to escort her to the bus-stop. It was early evening; as we passed by one local home, some of the large family were sitting outside enjoying the last rays of sun. The men were all very big, and the women were all married, except for one, who was unfortunately fat and ugly. One of the men in that family was married to a girl who lived next door to my mother. Another man - one of the fattest - had evidently returned home for a while from Bulawayo, where he earned his crust as a professional wrestler. He was unmarried, and that, too, was unsurprising - the guy seemed to share most of his genes with a hippo! Boy, with him and his sister around, it was enough to make you lose all of your appetite.

Anyway, they all greeted my mother and everything seemed to be fine. On our return, however, my sister and I found the wrestler and one of his brothers blocking our path in a particularly intimidating manner. All of a sudden, the fat man came towards me, grabbed me by the shoulders and attempted to kiss me. I wriggled away and started running towards their mother's house to report their bad behaviour; my younger sister followed quickly behind. Rushing to the kitchen, I blurted out the story but, before I could finish, the fat man came in and kicked me, pushing me out of the house and swearing and shouting at us, using terrible language. His mother and eldest brother simply stayed silent, watching their relative as he beat me up in their yard. The bastard even tried out some of his wrestling moves, and blood was soon pouring from my mouth where my lip had split open. My younger sister was screaming, and I was crying out, too, trying to force myself out of his grip. He paid no attention; if anything, our screams simply drove him on to kick me and punch me much harder. I got a glimpse of escape and tried to run away, but the fat man threw a bucket at my legs and I tripped and fell flat on my face.

When we finally got away, I was bruised and battered and my dress was badly torn. My sister and I went straight to the village headman's house to report the attack. This was when I realised the true level of antipathy that existed in the village towards me and my family; if anything, the headman seemed to think that the wrestler had done everyone a favour by beating me up. I was terrified by the experience and horrified by our apparent isolation. The next morning, mother took me straight to the village chairman and councillor to find out if there was any way that we could be helped. We also went to the wrestler's house; when questioned, he told my mother a pack of lies, which the people around him confirmed. The brute even claimed that I was his girlfriend, and had used him by taking a lot of his money to buy soft drinks and biscuits. I was too proud to accept him, they said; I had grown so arrogant since moving to the city to live with a Government Minister. This was! all crazy; I hardly even knew the man; the last time I'd seen him was when I was still a little girl at Sunday school and he was already a big guy who had come down to help out the teacher.

Naturally, I was hurt and disturbed by the lies. Mother saw through him, but the chairman and councillor, who I considered as almost a brother, seemed to believe the big fat man. I never spoke to his family again, and found it very hard to pass by their home without dredging up feelings of bitterness. By the time I got back to Harare, the Minister had already been informed about the incident; he questioned me about it at the weekend as we made our way out to the farm. There was something strange in his voice, something that went way beyond fatherly care. If anything, it sounded like jealousy; a few times on the journey, he made a point of stopping the car by the roadside, giving me a gentle touch on my leg or my face and saying how he had a very soft spot for me. I took this as his way of showing empathy, of letting me know how much he felt sorry for me in the light of my horrible experience. I was touched - in both senses of the word. It was on this journey that I also first noticed him wearing new aftershave - a lovely, comforting scent that went by the name of "Old Spice". The smell was so mesmerising and made me feel extremely relaxed around him; even a few days after we'd returned from the farm, I could still smell his presence around me. Yet I was unable to interpret any of this; I still showed the Minister the respect of a daughter and carried on with my regular duties.

One weekend, everything changed. We were at the farm, as usual, and I had just finished washing the dishes after supper. I went to the bathroom to start running his bath. When it was ready, I went to the office, where the Minister was sorting through papers, and told him the bath was now full. I went back to the kitchen to prepare the tea, but, just as I was taking it up to his room, I heard the Minister call. I put down the silver tray, went to the bathroom door and knocked softly. I didn't know what I had done, and was preparing myself for being told off. Instead, the Minister asked me to come in and start scrubbing his back with a bath stone. I felt so confused and embarrassed; this man was like a father to me -how could I look at his naked body in the bath? I had never bathed a big man before; in truth, I had never even glimpsed the naked body of one.

Before I could make sense of it all, the Minister called me again, this time in a commanding voice that almost made me jump. I opened the bathroom door; there he was, sitting in the bath tub, naked. I was shocked to see a man's body for the first time at such close range. I also quickly noticed that he had a few candles burning; their flames combined with the smell of the water in a strange hypnotising effect. My hands started to sweat, my knees trembled and my heart beat as fast as an African drum. For a second or two, I felt as if I might faint.

The Minister beckoned me other to the tub. Kneeling behind his back, I picked up the stone and started scrubbing it gently all over his skin. I was scared to look at his body; scared he might catch me. This lasted for what seemed like a lifetime. Each time he tried to talk, he would move his head in a manner that seemed to pull his whole body; I would quickly look away, or down to the floor, anywhere to avoid his eyes. Eventually, he told me to stop the scrubbing, and asked me to pass him the towel. Just as I was about to, he grabbed me and started to kiss me full on the mouth. My head span and my lips burnt. I could hear the sound of a thousand bells. Almost unable to stand up straight, I closed my eyes in total confusion. The kiss ended.

Before I could properly breathe, the Minister had carried me up to his room; I simply held on tight through fear. I suddenly realised that the towel wasn't around him and that his penis was shockingly hard. Gently laying me down on the bed, he almost seemed to apologise for what he was about to do. He said he would be able to explain everything afterwards. He said this as he leant over me, taking my clothes off at a remarkable rate. Within seconds, I was naked on his bed. The Minister started to lick me, and whisper unintelligible words in my ears. He said that he had fallen in love with me the moment he'd met me; that he'd been fantasising about the day we would finally make love. He promised to take care of me, to make me the happiest woman in the world. My nipples grew hard as his warm lips caressed them. I, too, started murmuring strange words that I could barely understand; I had no idea where they came from. I did tell him to stop and tried to push him away, but, all o! f a sudden, it just felt right. He was between my legs, pushing into my opening; there was a sharp crack, and the pain was excruciating. My life as a woman had started.

My future was being shaped in these moments; did I realise that my world would soon fall apart after experiencing what some women consider as bliss? I had endured abuse before, but this was no brutalised soldier. Or maybe it was. This man, like the others, thought he was taking my virginity. I didn't see it as such. Still now, despite the evidence of all of my children, I still think of myself as a virgin. I have never given myself freely to any man; my flesh may have been penetrated, but my soul never has.

The Minister made love to me the whole night, until he was too tired and I was too numb. In the morning, I awoke bruised and sore. He brought me breakfast in bed; as I nervously ate, he talked of his plans for our future together. He told me how his family had never taken to his wife; how he had tried to leave her behind in Europe, but how she had stubbornly followed, pregnant with their first son. Silently, I prayed he would not try to climb on top of me again.

We drove back to the city that evening. The Minister regularly squeezed my thighs with his hand; as we were approaching the house, he stopped the car and kissed me for what must have been a full five minutes. He whispered in my ear how much he was looking forward to our next weekend away. With the whisper came a warning:

if I was to tell anyone what had happened, my life would become a hell on earth. A shiver went down my spine.

When we entered the house, I excused myself quickly and went straight to my room. I felt soaked in guilt; it was as if everyone could tell what had happened. My life was now split: during the week, I was one of his children; at weekends, I was "darling", or "sweetheart", or whatever name he chose to call me. Sometimes, we would visit my mother together; by that point, word had spread and practically the whole Province knew of our relationship. My own family seemed to quietly approve; what else could they do? There was no one to complain to - we were dealing with a Government Minister, a Comrade, a man who decided who lived and who didn't. He was a power within himself, respected all across the nation.

I would arrive with him in the village, laden with all kinds of groceries; I was like the goddess of the family, and everyone showed me respect. I was growing into the role of the Minister's mistress, though it was always a fragile part to play. Day by day, I grew increasingly jealous of the Minister's wife, who he had repeatedly promised to leave. Day by day, I realised that this would never take place; that his love for me was little more than a whim, and that the power I'd assumed when our sex life had spread from the farm to the city - in secret, of course, while his wife was at work - was no more than a hollow and misplaced pride. Once, when his wife had come home early, the Minister had shoved me coldly in the wardrobe. I heard them talking, then watched them pick up from where we'd left off. When his wife had gone to the kitchen to make them some tea, the Minister ushered me naked out of his room; it was only luck that allowed me to get to my bedroom unseen. Late that night - almost at midnight - the Minister came up to check if I was alright. To him, the whole situation was no more than a joke. We made love, and I thought of his poor wife downstairs; for the first time, I began to feel sorry for her.

The situation was growing increasingly dangerous; even the Minister accepted as much, and decided we should meet in his office instead. We had lunchtime trysts on his big office desk, in the comfortable leather chairs, or in the back of his big black Mercedes; his drivers would be ordered home early, and we would head out towards the Hunyani River or the local forests. I was surprised that his wife never suspected; maybe she just didn't care.

Our affair had no effect on my studies; I progressed well and, after passing my secretarial course, the Minister found me a very good job as a Senior Staff Officer for the Special Constabulary. I had my own office, which I inherited from one of Harare's few remaining white officers: a man named Daniel, who left for South Africa with his family. I was now earning good money, so the Minister arranged for me to move out of his family house and in to one of his other big places in the Westwood region of town. The house he chose was one that he'd built himself; it had six bedrooms, a sitting room, dining room and very big fitted kitchen. It stood on a hill, with views as far as the eye could see. I loved it as soon as I saw it.

On weekends, we would still generally go to the farm, though sometimes the Minister would take me on trips, out to Victoria Falls, or Kariba, or the Great Zimbabwe ruins, where he claimed that his ancestors came from. On occasions, he would come to my house late at night and we would share a few hours before he returned to his wife. Our relationship remained a secret, if perhaps not a perfectly kept one. To the outside world, I was still very much the Minister's daughter, not lover; this pretence, he said, was the only way to secure his job and not break the heart of his wife. He maintained that she should never find out until he was ready to announce our love to the world; that, he said, would happen soon enough, though I never really placed faith in his words. I accepted myself as a bit on the side and started to plan my way out. Pregnancy stood in my way.

The Minister was furious; he ordered me to resign from my job, and insinuated that the child wasn't his; in his mind, I had been sleeping with the Rasta manager of a band of English musicians who had rented out one of his offices. He warned me never to come to his office, and quickly arranged for another family to rent out a large part of the house, confining me to one room at the top and a share of the bathroom and kitchen. The new man of the house was a custom and excise officer and his wife was a senior sister at Harare Hospital. They had a dog and a child, and a lot of their relatives used to come and visit for what seemed like forever. They brought rules to the house, and treated me in much the same way as a servant; whenever there were chores to be done, it was me who was asked, especially if there were visitors around to impress. Sometimes, they even locked the bathroom door at night for no reason, and I had to sneak out into the garden. Things couldn't have been much worse if the Minister had specifically asked them to torture and tease me, which I had a feeling he might well have done. If he was trying to drive me way, he would have to try harder; after all, there was no place else for me to go - unemployed and pregnant, my family no longer seemed so keen to see me.

I was abandoned. The Minister offered me one final chance; I could take two hundred dollars to a doctor's surgery in Manica Road and get an abortion. When I refused, telling him I would rather die than murder an innocent child, he reacted with terrible anger, screaming all kinds of names and hurling the money in my face. That night, I cried myself to sleep.

The money kept me fed for a while, but when it ran out I had little idea where to find my next meal. On rare occasions, the Minister would come to collect his rent; if he saw me, he would throw me some money as if at a dog or a beggar. Sometimes, he would send me on errands, ordering me to pick up the rents from his various tenants, including those musicians from England. They were the only ones who showed any affection, and I would stay in their studio for most of the day. I had nothing else to do. The name of their band was "Misty and Roots", and their manager was indeed a man that I liked, though nothing had happened between us. I longed for the musicians to take me back with them to England; this was my only potential ticket to freedom. They were good people, and I felt sure they would provide well for me and my baby, although I hadn't yet said I was pregnant; I still didn't want to expose either the Minister or myself.

The band played shows all over Harare; I would often go to watch, then join them for a meal before hurrying back over to Westwood, where the gate and front door would always be locked. Those nights I slept outside, curled up with the dog for warmth. As I felt the baby quietly kicking, I would look up at the sky and count the shooting stars. In the morning, I would wake to the sound of the husband's car and rush to the kitchen door before his wife had had time to lock it again.

Once, when I came back to the house after completing my errands, I was surprised to find a group of visitors awaiting me. It was my uncle Jo - my mother's eldest brother - and his wife, come over from England. Jo had left Zimbabwe - or what was then Rhodesia - in the Sixties and hadn't been back. He was a very dark man and as tall as a giant; his wife was South African, and she was very beautiful indeed. Apparently, before she had married my uncle, she had been one of the mistresses of King Sobhusa of Swaziland. Her name was Indlovhukhazi, which translates as female elephant. Jo, too, had his stories; he had abandoned his country for political reasons; his father had been chief of his province and, upon his death, Jo had been violently threatened by local rivals. He was now a very well-educated man, with a clutch of degrees, who worked as a minister of the church; I heard him preach once, on the subject of Moses and the burning bush, and it was one of the most moving experiences in my life. Jo really had the gift to change people for the better; he was so good he could have made even the devil repent for his sins.

Naturally, I was extremely happy to see such wonderful relatives; I threw myself into my uncle's outstretched arms and cried uncontrollably. Jo was shocked to see I was pregnant; as I told him the story, he grew very angry and demanded that I accompany him and his wife to the Minister's house. I tried my best to dissuade him, but Jo was insistent, and I reluctantly led them to the big white house out in the Highlands.

When we arrived in the early evening, the Minister was not yet at home; his wife was clearly surprised to see me, even more so when she saw I was pregnant. Sparing no details, Jo immediately told her the purpose of our visit; as the depth of her betrayal was revealed, pain and anger spread over her face; by the time we left, tears were streaming down her face. Jo's parting shot was a strong warning to be given to the Minister: if he didn't support me, Jo would take him to court and make him pay for the rest of his life.

After that, things improved, at least for a while. The Minister refused to meet Jo, but did start sending me money for food, and would even occasionally stop in to see that I was doing alright. This didn't please the other tenants, who took to visiting the Minister's office and feeding him lies about how I brought men home at night; how one of the musicians had become my new lover; and how I had started drinking alcohol and smoking marijuana and generally behaving in a terrible manner. What hurt most was that the Minister chose to believe all these lies, despite the fact that, deep down, he must have known I was incapable of doing such things. Not that it stopped him from visiting me and sleeping with me whenever he liked, almost up to the day I gave birth.

The night that I went into labour, I was alone at home and the streets seemed deserted. As the pains grew, I walked slowly next door and borrowed their phone to call the Minister, who eventually arrived, looking angry and grim, and drove me to a clinic in Kambuzuma. At the gates of the clinic, he asked me to get out of the car; when I did so, he pulled round and sped off back home.

I rang the bell at the gate. The midwife came out and was very surprised to see me on my own with no baby bag and no hospital notes. I lived in the same house as a senior midwife, but she had never even asked how I was feeling, let alone suggested that I should attend an ante-natal clinic.

With the baby clearly on its way, the midwife at Kambuzuma had no choice but to admit me, with or without the right papers. I spent the whole night in labour and gave birth to a healthy baby boy at about quarter to ten the next morning. I was a mother, and overwhelmed with all kinds of emotions. I could breastfeed my baby, but could I support him? I had no clothes for him; when the midwife discharged me, she offered two blankets to wrap round his body. Still feeling tender and fragile, I carried the baby all the way back to Westwood. Later that evening, the Minister's driver arrived with two hundred dollars and a message that I was to return to my village immediately. That was the closest I got to congratulations; I felt more like I'd committed a crime than just given birth to a beautiful baby.

The next day, instead of catching the bus to my village as ordered, I took a trip to the shopping centre in Kambuzuma, where I bought a few things for the baby and a few groceries for myself. I took them home to await the Minister's next move; I was determined to stay in his house until my little boy had grown up - surely he owed me that much!

Things went silent for over three months and my purse was growing dangerously close to empty. One day, while I was feeding the baby, I heard the Minister's car pull up outside of the house. My first thought was that he had come to see the baby and bring me some money; perhaps he had finally come to his senses! How stupid and naive I still was! The Minister was in no mood to coo over his son; angrily, he ordered me to pack up all of my clothes - if I refused to go to my village by bus, then he would damn well take me there himself! He warned me that he had gathered enough evidence to prove that I was not as straight-forward a girl as I seemed; naturally, the only witness was the custom and excises officer that I lived with.

Mouth open in shock and despair, I could summon no words to defend myself; what would have been the point of arguing with two people who had already judged and condemned me. It seemed that the final act of crucifixion would take place in front of my mother. Surrendered to my fate, I quickly packed my bag and joined the Minister and his witness in the back of the big black Mercedes. The engine was already running. At that moment, I saw through the Minister's motives, why he was doing things in so much of a hurry. He simply didn't want to think through the course of his actions. Every time I looked at him, he resolutely avoided my eyes; when I sat in the back of the car, he adjusted his mirror so that he wouldn't accidentally catch my eye. Is a bully always aware of his guilt?

My mother was reduced to nothing. The Minister threatened to call a huge rally, telling everyone how she had raised a loose daughter, who had now taken to accusing decent people like him of getting her pregnant. I had no idea that politics could play such an important role at the level of sex and babies, but what surprised me most of all was the way in which the Minister could sit in my mother's Nyore-nyore chair, drinking sweet tea and eating her homemade biscuits, while making these horrible threats. At one point, he even pretended to cry at the very same time as stuffing his mouth with a crispy brown cookie. It was a pathetic and embarrassing display - the cruellest and most degrading act since Judas' moment of glory! Even the custom and excise officer seemed uncomfortable, fidgeting silently and avoiding all eye contact as the Minister kept referring to him as a witness and hinting at all the filthy tales my mother could hear if only we had enough time.

My innocence couldn't prevent me from wishing the ground would swallow me up. It was only the sight of my baby that convinced me that things would work out; the boy was almost a carbon copy of his father, who now stood here, loudly rejecting the child in front of my mother. As the baby started to cry, I brought out my breast and silently started to feed him. The room fell quiet; even the Minister had run out of words, and sweat was now dripping from his forehead. The big bowl of fat cooks was now almost empty; the pig had practically eaten them all.

After a period of silence, my mother asked the Minister if she could pray before he left; he agreed, and fear was etched across his face as mother spoke words that came deep from her heart, thanking God for the baby, for the Minister and his witness, for my health and the fact that we had all been brought together in her home. She asked God to guide the Minister and his witness on their journey back home, and to intervene in the situation that had been presented to her. When she finished, she thanked the Minister for bringing her daughter home. Not at one single point did she utter a word against the Minister and his witness; they left for the city with their tails between their legs.

When they were gone, mother took the baby in her arms and began to pray again. This time, she could no longer hold back the tears as she rocked the baby gently and kissed his little head. I suffered her pain and sobbed uselessly, wondering what was to become of us all.

CHAPTER 13

There was not enough food to feed the baby; my left breast would no longer bring any milk. He became very sick, developing kwashiorkor, which caused his skin to peel off and him to suffer from terrible diarrhoea. Mother worked extremely hard to nurse the baby back to health. The three of us struggled as the villagers gossiped and laughed. There was a point when it seemed he wouldn't make it; hope was running low, but mother prayed day and night, asking God to have mercy on the baby's innocent soul. At night, I could hear mother crying; I felt useless, and desperately cast around for a plan. There was only one thing for it: I would go back to the big city and face up to the Minister - his threats couldn't scare me or keep me away!

One morning, I told mother that I had to go back to Harare to gather what little furniture I owned so we could sell it to help feed the baby. I boarded the bus and didn't pay for my ticket; it was one of the Minister's buses, and the driver and conductor still thought of me as his mistress. I even asked the conductor to give me some money from the takings, lying to him that the Minister had told me to do so. When we arrived at Mbare Market, he gave me three hundred dollars and I took a taxi straight back to my old house in Westwood.

Fortunately, the customs and excise officer and his wife had moved out; I introduced myself to the new tenants - a Baptist minister, his lovely wife and four children - who were only too happy to let me back in.

After a few days, I felt confident enough to tell them the whole of the story; having heard of my woes, the churchman assured me that nothing bad would happen so long as he was around. The Minister himself was soon aware of my reappearance, but this time he chose to ignore it. Even when he came to inspect the house, he simply shook his head when he saw me, and silently passed on by. This was a battle I'd finally won.

My plan was to find a job and start sending money back to my mother in the village. As always, I had a strong desire to continue my education, but had to think of a way that wouldn't eat into my funds. Mother was worried; the baby had very little to eat or wear, and there was pressure on me to act fast. Thankfully, the church minister and his family added me into their budget, so I didn't have to think about buying my food. All they asked in return was that I attended their evening prayers and occasionally accompanied them to church, where we would spend the whole day singing, studying the Bible and worshiping until there was nothing left to say or confess. At the end of such days, we would all pile into their big red Pontiac, which poured smoke from its broken exhaust as we drove noisily back through the city.

Other habits developed. On Thursdays, I would always join the family to watch "Mvengemvenge", a kind of mix-and-match version of "Top of the Pops", which featured an eclectic range of musicians displaying their talents. "Mr Mukadota" would follow; this was a very humorous and educational show, which I had watched plenty of times at the Minister's house. It focused on the everyday problems faced by families in Zimbabwe, of which I had had my fair share. I soon developed a burning ambition to appear in the show and decided to write to its manager, who also took care of a popular band called "Safirio Madzikatire". Within a week of my letter, the manager himself was standing by the big gate of my house, calling my name and surrounded by all of the church minister's children. When I came out, he smiled at my appearance and said he would introduce me to Mr Mukadota's producer, who would have the final say on whether I could appear in the show.

This was all wonderful news; it felt like the heavens had opened and, that night, I slept like a log. The next day, the manager picked me up and drove me over to the studios of Zimbabwe Broadcasting Corporation. The producer, a tall handsome man, looked me over with approval, and was impressed with my level of English. They were looking for someone to act as a the wife of Bonnie, an old professor who had turned alcoholic. I seemed to fit the shoes well, and was soon learning my lines and getting to know all the rest of the group. Soon enough, I was on national TV, on my way to celebrity status and picking up two hundred and fifty dollars for my very first night's work. Things were looking up!

The next morning, I rushed to the bus terminal with the money and a letter for my mother, telling her how lucky I'd been. It was soon clear that she didn't share my enthusiasm for the new work; at that time in Zimbabwe, being an actress was strongly associated with prostitution. My mother was very angry indeed, but we needed the money so she couldn't complain when I sent it. With some that I had left over, I was able to finance a return to Species College, enrolling for A-Levels in English Language, History and Religious Education. I also took up Pitman's Shorthand again; I hadn't quite mastered it in my earlier course.

By now, I had made a few friends in the Westwood region; the best were two guys called Graham Nhidza, who looked after me like a brother, and Aaron Chiundura Moyo, who loved books and lived in Kambuzuma. Aaron was a prominent Zimbabwean author, who had written lots and lots of books. I remember the time we spent hours and hours in his house - which was more like a library - discussing a controversial play called "Caught in the crossfire". Aaron was much older than me, but he often acted as if he was younger. Graham was more into movies than books; he would sometimes take me to catch a film in the city centre. One time, we went to see a Brooke Shields movie called "Endless Love". Its romance brought tears to my eyes, though Graham just laughed. He later became an army officer in the King George VI regiment. Neither Graham nor Aaron ever seemed to have a girlfriend; I never thought to ask them why.

One day after filming, I arrived back home to find the church minister waiting for me by the gate. He told me that a big black Mercedes beside had pulled up in our drive and two people had been asking to see me. My first impulse was fear, but things were far from as bad as they seemed; the car did, indeed, belong to a minister, but the Minister for Education, not the one for Home Affairs. His bodyguard and driver had come to collect me; for unknown reasons, the Minister for Education had requested my presence in his office downtown.

I'd met the man on several occasions - he was very close friends with my former lover - the two of them considered themselves the best-educated men in the Government, aside, of course, from President Mugabe, who held a whole clutch of doctorates and degrees. The Minister for Education knew the whole story about how I had come to live with his colleague, how I had been taken in and adopted as a daughter, though whether he knew more I had little idea. He himself was a former freedom fighter, with an air of kindness but a very short temper. He was also a single man - one of the very few government ministers who still wasn't married - though it was widely rumoured he had fathered a child during the war. The Minister for Education wasn't a very attractive man, nor did he have any idea how to dress; for the most part, he still wore combat clothes, and was very rarely to be seen in a suit.

The churchman handed me twenty dollars left by the Minister's messengers alongside instructions for me to come to the Ministry of Education at ten o'clock the very next day. I had little choice but to comply; curiosity was already killing me and I couldn't wait to find out why I'd been called. The churchman promised to pray for me while I was out; he didn't seem worried, so neither was I. He was a good man of God, who always offered me comfort when things took a turn. Who knew which direction my life was now heading?

The next day, I put on my lovely green polka-dot dress and some nice sandals that I'd bought at the Bata shop in the city. I took a taxi to Manica Road and walked past the Central Police Station towards the Ambassador Hotel, where the Ministry of Education was based. The security guard had been expecting me, and ushered me into the lift, which shuttled me up a couple of floors to the office of the Minister's private secretary. She had a whole bunch of files in her hands and was evidently about to leave as soon as I arrived; she pointed me into the Minister's office and I entered to find him smiling up from his seat on a big leather sofa. He was holding a pen and somehow smelled of a good education.

I moved as if to kneel down before him, but instead found myself pulled into a hug, crushed against his bear-like chest. The Minister held me close for a good few seconds, laughing and exuding some strange kind of sympathy. He said he'd been angry to hear what had happened between me and his colleague; he wondered out loud how a man in control of his senses could possibly treat such a beautiful woman in such an irresponsible manner. He also said that he'd seen me on TV; he demanded to know why I'd had to sink so low. I told him it was a way of paying my fees and helping my mother to care for my baby.

The conversation became ever more revealing. The Minister said that his friend and colleague the Minister for Home Affairs had promised him that I would become his girlfriend; that he and I had been cruelly misled; but that, despite what had happened, he was still prepared to take me as his wife. How very romantic! The Minister even explained that he had asked his secretary to leave

DEBRA CHIDAKWA

for the day so that he could have some quality time with his new lover - me. He told me all this in as matter-of-fact a manner as if he were ordering food in a restaurant.

Sat there on his sofa, I thought of all the beautiful romances I'd read of in my "Mills and Boon" novels; how the man would gently ask out the lady; how their relationship would slowly blossom like the flowers that he regularly gave her; how their first kiss would shake the earth. How the man would select only the choicest of moments to propose to his beautiful lover; how she would cry while slipping on her new ring; and how their fairy-tale wedding would be followed by a tropical honeymoon and a lifetime of happiness. Was that kind of romance no more than a fiction? To this day, I'm not sure it exists.

My new ministerial companion broke the tension by offering to take me out for lunch. I was still speechless and stunned, with little idea what to do and a horrible sense of what was to come - something that I wasn't prepared to go through again. Sure enough, the Minister was soon all over me; he was a very heavy man and his powerful hugs made me feel as if hot coals of fire had been lodged in my chest. He squeezed my breasts in a particularly rough manner, and his prickly moustache scratched against my cheek whenever I pulled away from his cold sloppy kisses. His

220

saliva almost choked me, but the Minister seemed to be having his fun, judging by the ecstatic groans and grunts that emerged from his throat. My thighs felt ice-cold; in fact, the whole of my body was covered in pimples. Thankfully, it was all over soon; ever the romantic, the Minister simply told me to wash myself down in his bathroom.

I scrubbed hard all over my body, sobbing quietly and feeling so dirty and useless. The Minister himself suddenly entered the room, muttering something about cleaning his "drilling machine". He asked me to hurry; he had already summoned his driver to take us for lunch. My appetite was gone, but the Minister was apparently ravenous. In his car on the way back to Westwood, he informed me that, as I was now practically his wife, he no longer wanted to see me appear on TV. It was degrading, he said, and, anyway, he would take good care of me now. His driver and bodyguard would come to check on me each day, as if I were a precious gem that needed protecting. I had no strength to challenge what was said and done on that day. How could I have protested; I'd heard enough of pretty young girls mysteriously disappearing after sordid affairs with a government minister. People knew what was happening behind those big office walls, but very few dared to announce it.

True to his word, the Minister sent his driver and guard round to my house the very next morning.

They arrived with bags full of groceries, a few items of clothing and an expensive bottle of perfume from Greatermans, one of the best shops in the city. The church minister, who I had come to trust, claimed that all would work out well if only I kept my mouth quiet. It was strange to hear a man of the cloth saying something as vile as that; he should have known better, and perhaps should have saved me from the snares of the devil.

The Minister for Education started sending me money, which I mainly passed on to my mother. One day, out of the blue, he announced that he had found me a job as a temporary teacher at a school in Kadoma. When he told me which one, I just couldn't believe it; I was to be installed as a new teacher at Zhombe Mission School - the very place where Mama Kuda had worked while I'd been taking care of her baby all those years ago. To go with the job, I would get a fully furnished house, complete with electricity and fresh water supply! It was almost unbelievable! What's more, the Minister's very own uncle was the area's education welfare officer, and he had sworn to look after me well. The Minister himself said he would visit as often as possible; in his fast and comfortable Mercedes, the journey would not be so difficult.

I arranged for the removal of what little furniture I owned from the house in Westwood; my bed, my flowery table and chairs were all sent back to my mother's village. I was finally set to move away from the city that had grown into my home, and away from the people - Graham, Aaron, the church minister's family - who had grown into my friends. It was time to move on with my life.

CHAPTER 14

I arrived at mother's house while the sun was still strong. Taking my son in my arms, I watched the removal men unload the few things that I owned from the back of their van. Mother seemed strangely sad and concerned; each time that I caught her eye, I could feel there was something that she wanted to ask me.

We put away the furniture, then sat down to a meal in silence. Mother cleared her throat; perhaps now she was ready to talk. Turning directly to me, she asked if I was feeling alright. I replied that everything was fine; I could see that this wasn't the answer she'd wanted. She then asked me to tell her more about the Minister of Education. With little hesitation, I told her how wonderful he was, how he had found me a great job in Kadoma, and how fast I was growing to love him. Mother didn't seem at all impressed; she simply asked me again if everything was alright. Confused, I asked her what she meant; she responded by asking if I'd noticed any changes to my body. Well, yes, perhaps I'd gained a bit of weight, and maybe I'd missed a period or two, but that was fairly normal; grandmother had once told me that such gaps were all part of the cycle, something she referred to as "fundisi". I repeated that I was fine, and said how much I was looking forward to starting my job. She told me she thought I was pregnant; that the signs were all over my body.

Call me stupid; call me naive. Call me what you will. I had noticed nothing. I'd been through all the same little changes the first time around, but my mind couldn't - or perhaps didn't want to - make the clear-cut connection. That night, I slept very badly; the prospect of having a second child out of wedlock was not extremely appealing. In fact, it was plain frightening, no matter how many times I assured myself that this time would be different; that my man loved me and would take care of his baby.

The next morning, we woke at half five and began the twenty-mile trip to the local clinic in Mbiri, where I would find out for sure if I was pregnant or not. The clinic was surrounded by shops and a few grinding mills; before reaching it, we also passed by the surgery of Dr Kaunda, our local G.P., who was well-known and respected throughout the Nhema region. Dr Kaunda was good with injections, and renowned for his treatment of measles and mumps; many songs were sung by the people of Nhema about all his good works and contribution to health. In fact, Mbiri was home to many of the most famous residents of our province; people like Chief Nhema and his successor Dhayidhayi, Reverend Fundira

and his wife, who had become a leader for all of
our women; and Chiware, the Chief of Police.
There were plenty of others, too: Honondo, the
master farmer; Chakamanga, the popular butcher;
Matiyasi, the giant; and Sadhibha Terry, the dip-
tank supervisor with the legendary ability to
seduce women through the tunes of his whip.
Walking to the clinic in Mbiri was like taking a stroll
down Sunset Boulevard!

We arrived at the clinic around ten o'clock,
finding the sister in charge at the end of a nice cup
of tea. My mother knew this lady; after a brief
conversation, I was handed a paper tray in the
shape of an oversized bean and ushered off to the
bathroom to provide a small sample of urine for
testing. Mother seemed lost in thought as we
waited for the sister to confirm my result; when
she did - and said that it was positive, and that I
was most definitely pregnant - mother instantly
burst into tears. Dear God, what had I done now?

We thanked the good sister and headed back
home. As soon as we were out of the centre of
Mbiri, away from the shops and in the shade of
some bushes, mother asked if we could sit down
and talk. We did, and it lasted a while; mother
clearly expressed disappointment, and suggested
that, if it was true that the Minister loved me, the
best thing to do was for me to head back to Harare
and tell him. Within our culture, if a girl became
pregnant it was tradition to go to the house of the

unborn baby's father and perform certain rituals, including the payment of a bridal price, known as "lobola". After our talk, mother began praying to God for advice and protection. I had let her down once again, but things were not lost. The Minister of Education was a prominent, respectable man in our government; surely he wouldn't abandon a pregnant young lover. With this belief, mother and I rebuilt our brittle confidence; how quickly and conveniently we come to forget the sad lessons of experience.

The very next morning, I said my farewells and took the early Marongwe bus to Harare. I'd reached Mbare Market by one, and took a taxi straight into the city. At the Ambassador Hotel, I was told that the Minister for Education had very recently returned to his office after a meeting with the President. He seemed happy to see me and suggested we head out for lunch at the airport hotel. I knew what that meant: food followed by a lengthy siesta that could last for the whole of the night.

As it turned out, I stayed at the hotel not only that night, but the whole of the week. When I told the Minister of my pregnancy he betrayed little emotion, showing no signs of either anger or excitement. He simply changed the subject. His reaction surprised me, but I took comfort in the thought that he hadn't abandoned me; if he had no longer been interested, he could easily have walked off with no questions asked. At the end of the week, the Minister told me that the plans for Kadoma would still go ahead; this would give him time to approach the President and explain that we wanted to marry. The Minister was keen to avoid media meddling in his private affairs and felt it was best for me to be out of Harare. When we were married, I could return and be formally introduced as the wife of the Minister of Education - how very dignified! This all seemed fine by me; in fact, it felt like my prayers had been answered.

With money from the Minister, I went shopping in the big department stores of the city and set up accounts at both a bank and a building society. My future husband proved extremely generous, and I could now buy all that I needed, as well as send money home to my mother. Whenever I went to the Minister's office, he would unlock a small drawer, pull out a fistful of dollars and hand it to me without even counting. With all his support, it wouldn't be a problem for me to perform the traditional duty of offering my first month's salary as thanksgiving to my mother.

When the time came for me to leave for Kadoma, the Minister explained that he wouldn't be able to escort me as he was due overseas for an extremely important conference in Geneva. This kind of thing was a regular occurrence; all prominent ministers travelled abroad, and I was always excited to see him appear on the news, especially one time, when he was in England, and white snow was falling softly upon his dark head. It made me proud that the father of my baby was such a significant figure, and such a fine gentleman too! He was a freedom fighter, a man who had survived in the bush before rising up to become head of education for the whole of our country. I should have guessed he was a wonderful liar and schemer.

Instead, I waved goodbye to the man of my dreams on a Saturday morning, and was taken off by his driver to my new destination. The Minister had left me with a kiss on the cheek and a big brown envelope packed full of money - no less than two thousand dollars, all fresh from the mint! I was sad to be parting, but comforted myself that we would soon be together, united by law. How could I have guessed that this would be the last time I saw him in person for close on twenty years? The next time we met was in the UK, when the Minister was there on a visit. By then, though, he was no longer the Minister for Education in Zimbabwe; he was Deputy Manager of the World Bank, and living comfortably in Washington D.C.

The Minister's uncle, who was known as Mr R.B.K., lived in a beautiful house in Zhombe Tribal Trust Land. When we arrived at noon on that Saturday, he warmly welcomed me and quickly introduced me to his children. For some reason, he insisted on calling me Sarah; this was particularly strange since he seemed to know so much about me. I later discovered that the Minister's driver had conveyed this name to Mr R.B.K. in secret, supposedly as part of a plan to stop any journalists hunting me down. I accepted it easily enough; after all, it was far from the first time I'd adapted my name.

The kitchen of the house was extraordinarily big; at meal times, all the family would gather round its fire for food and entertainment. Sometimes, a scorpion would fall from the thatch and all hell would break loose; everyone was justifiably scared of a scorpion's sting, which could inflict the most terrible pain. It was believed that the quickest way to kill the pain was to murder the creature itself; if it was allowed to live, the pain would simply spread as it scuttled around. The other traditional remedy was to cut open the skin and let the poison bleed out, although Mr R.B.K. also had a herbal potion that apparently offered some comfort.

The rest of his home consisted of two well-furnished cottages, complete with dining rooms, lounges and shiny white toilets. In fact, everything was very modern and comfortable. As I mentioned before, Mr R.B.K. was the education welfare officer for Kadoma province; he was paid very well and had plenty of cattle and goats. His ex-wife, a teacher, had contributed greatly to creating their luxurious home; it was a shame she had been driven to alcoholism and kicked out of the house.

The Minister's bodyguard and driver stayed with us for dinner - delicious sadza and chicken - then headed off back to Harare. As they left, they promised to return with the Minister as soon as he'd come back from Geneva. Mr R.B.K. took me on a tour of his home, then led me down to a field he owned that was overflowing with fluffy white cotton. He told me my things had been taken to the second cottage near the kitchen; one of its big bedrooms with fitted wardrobes would be mine.

The room was extremely well-furnished, with a zebra-skin rug at the foot of the bed. There was a small wireless radio, with an extra pack of batteries beside in case the current ones ran out. The massive wooden bed had fresh sheets and blankets and pillows; boy, did it look welcoming - I only wished that the Minister could be here to share it! I lay down on the bed and imagined waking to the cooing of doves in the tree tops outside, and the lowing of cows as they provided fresh milk for my breakfast. When Mr R.B.K. knocked at the door, I was practically asleep, but he soon cleared my head by telling me to always check my blankets before getting into the bed - who knows what scorpions or snakes might be hoping to sleep there!

That evening, right after supper, Mr R.B.K. told me about Empress Mine, the school I was going to teach in. It was a big secondary school, which took its name from the steel mines that surrounded it. The army's famous fifth brigade was actually based at the school, and there was a big clinic with an army dentist who was famously good at extracting teeth. Empress Mine wasn't far from Zhombe Mission School, where Mama Kuda had worked. After his little lecture, Mr R.B.K. unexpectedly gave me a payslip, complete with my name and details of my first salary of seven hundred dollars; it seemed I had got on the payroll without even stepping foot in the school! What pleased me the most was that my real was written on the payslip; no matter what people called me, I could still keep my identity intact.

I was due to start the job on Monday, so on the Sunday morning Mr R.B.K. took me to meet the head teacher of Empress Mine. On the way, he warned me not to mention the Minister at all; he looked more serious than I'd seen him before, and it was clear that he meant what he said. The head teacher turned out to be a very warm and welcoming man, though he was clearly somewhat ill at ease to be visited by the important education officer - Mr R.B.K. was effectively his boss. He gave a great performance, speaking in English all the way through, despite the fact that all three of us could speak better Shona. It seemed that I would be teaching English Language and Literature, as well as supervising netball training and providing classes in Personal Hygiene to the higher-grade female students, some of whom were actually older than my eldest sister. These girls were returnees, who had abandoned school during the war to help serve the freedom fighters. Some had had fatherless children, and I recognised my own struggles in the pain I saw etched on their faces. They were young women and mothers, but, at school, they were still on a level with children; unsurprisingly, a certain level of hostility flowed through their veins.

The Minister of Education had proposed free education for all, opening the floodgates for anyone interested to come back to school. Unsurprisingly, there was a shortage of trained teachers; anyone with five O-Levels or more was eligible to become a temporary teacher. With my A-Levels and administrative qualifications, I was in an even better position than most fully-qualified teachers. I knew my books and could recite whole passages from *Things Fall Apart, The River Between, Dew in the Morning, Romeo and Juliet* and *Hard Times* as if I had written them myself. I especially loved *Romeo and Juliet* - it was the most romantic and heartbreaking story that I'd ever read. I used to ask myself what I would do if I fell in love with someone like Romeo and my parents refused to bless our relationship. How touching and sad it was that two people had to surrender their lives as proof of their love. I promised myself that all my students would benefit from the lessons of literature, and that whoever came across my teaching would come away with something special.

Thankfully, that's how things largely turned out; I know of two of my students who went on to be doctors, as well as many who became nurses and teachers or responsible husbands and housewives. My netball coaching also proved up to the task - the Empress Mine team won many a trophy - while the good reputation of my cookery classes soon spread throughout the whole Zhombe region; local village women would often ask me to teach them to bake the legendary fat cooks that I had learnt from my mother. In fact, people started coming to me for advice on all kinds of matters. My capabilities surprised even me, and my success in the classroom kept me going despite all the problems outside.

Being at school was once again the highlight of my day; returning home to Mr R.B.K.'s, there would always be a pile of work waiting for me, whether it was dealing with the cotton, cooking for the family, or cleaning the cottages. By now, I was heavily pregnant, and the weather wasn't helping my cause - Zhombe had become as hot as hell. The nearest ante-natal clinic was about a five-kilometre walk through deep forest; the journey would blister my feet and, occasionally, my pelvis would seem to seize up, forcing me to rest under the shade of one of the many trees.

On certain days, I would come across a few local villagers making their way to the grinding mill at Sidhakeni, accompanied by oxen pulling scotch-carts heavily laden with big bags of maize. They would kindly invite to travel on top of their carts, and I would clamber up over the bags to find a not too uncomfortable position in which to sit. It was always a bumpy ride, but far better than walking. On arrival, I would hand the villagers a few dollars, which they happily and rapidly spent on biscuits and drinks. One man was so grateful that he immediately offered to give me a lift on his bicycle whenever I had an appointment; all he asked for in exchange was a bottle of Fanta and a couple of buns. When I politely refused his kind offer, disappointment was written all over his face; I ended up giving him five dollars that day to stave off my strange sense of guilt.

During the long hot months in Zhombe, I never saw the Minister once. Then, one day, the head teacher of Empress Mine announced in assembly that the Minister of Education would be visiting Zhombe Mission and that all of the surrounding schools were required to attend. Finally, I'd get a chance to confront him and find out how he could have forgotten my existence. When the day of the visit arrived, I put on my best maternity dress and set out early to make sure that I got a good seat. There was really no way he could miss me; I was sat right at the front, my big belly right under his nose.

The Minister saw me, alright; he simply refused to speak; even his driver and bodyguard walked past me without saying a word. How dare he just treat me like that - it felt like everyone knew what was happening, like I was being formally dumped in front of hundreds of school kids and teachers! I was left utterly humiliated, sick to the stomach with the thought of having been left in the lurch once again. How obvious it had been that the bastard was destined to leave me! How could I have been so stupid as to let myself fall into the exact same trap twice!

Late the following Friday afternoon, Mr R.B.K. told me that the Minister was about to get married. Indeed, the wedding was set for the very next day; it had apparently been all over the news, but the batteries for my radio had long since gone flat. If I had known, there was no way I would have attended the Minister's speech; the bastard had left me numb and heartbroken: what could I have done to deserve this? Mr R.B.K. was attending the wedding, as was the President and many prominent government officials, including ministers from overseas. It was all I could do to stay mute as he told me; later that night, I cried uncontrollably until the tears had run dry from my eyes. I wrote a very painful letter to my mother; I knew she would be devastated. I also knew that my time in Mr R.B.K.'s home would soon be reaching its end. I made plans to move out right after the birth, which was due now in less than a month.

There were some houses in the army camp that were specially reserved for teachers; they were very well built, with a good water supply and electricity, and didn't cost a penny. On the day of the Minister's wedding, I went to see the head teacher at Empress Mine and confided in him my whole story. As it turned out, he already knew; a student of his, who was now training as a teacher at Belvedere College in Harare, had informed him of the rumours. The head teacher, such a kind man, promised me that, by the time the baby was born, a place would be ready for me in one of the teachers' residences.

My relationship with Mr R.B.K. quickly deteriorated. After he had told me about the Minister's wedding, I uncovered a whole trail of deceit and realised he'd played a key part in the conspiracy against me. I felt cheated and used, and could no longer trust him; when I started to go into labour, early one September morning, I refused to tell either him or his children. At first, I simply ignored the pains, but my breathing was growing increasingly heavy and the heat was becoming unbearable. One of Mr R.B.K's girls must have seen my distress; she came knocking on my bedroom door to check if I was alright.

The moment she opened the door, my waters broke; the baby was now ready to come out! Obviously, there was no time to go the clinic; there'd be no qualified mid-wife at this birth. The girl rushed out of my bedroom and frantically called out to her father in the fields, where he was working alongside the village headman's wife. They both came running back up to the house, where they found me busy pushing. Suddenly, all manner of chaos broke out: at the foot of my bed, a huge snake appeared out of nowhere, uncoiling itself like a rope. My god, it was big, and obviously attracted by the scent of fresh blood - the damn creature was after my baby! I screamed and pushed with a powerful force, inspired by equal doses of fear and pain. There was a gun shot, then the sound of a baby's first cries; I looked up to see the headman's wife holding my child, and Mr R.B.K. standing at the foot at the bed with a pistol in his hand. He had shot the snake point blank in the head; had he missed! , who knows what would have happened! One of his daughters came rushing in with a bowl of hot water and a razor to cut the umbilical cord. My room had become like a slaughter house; the smell of the snake's blood mixed with my own was horrific!

As soon as the baby's cord had been cut and tied, the headman's wife brought her over for me to hold. She was so beautiful; it seemed almost as though she were smiling. The story of her dramatic birth soon spread all over Zhombe, and people came up to tell me of its significance, how it meant that the baby would grow into a great and special person. That, of course, was always nice to hear, though I never liked to be reminded of the day of the birth itself; afterwards, I refused to spend another night in my previous room; instead, I asked Mr R.B.K if I could sleep on floor in one of his own daughters' bedrooms. I was ready to be stung by a scorpion if it meant not having to sleep in that blood-stained bedroom.

About a week later, when I'd re-gathered some of my strength, I took the baby to the clinic for her first full check up. It was a difficult journey - walking for miles under the heat of the sun and the weight of my newborn child - but it was worth it to hear she was well. On my return, I summoned the courage to tell Mr R.B.K I was leaving his house. He was angry to lose me as I'd become like a servant, or house girl, for him and his family; he started accusing me of hoping to move in with a man on the Empress Mine estate, even going so far as to ridiculously suggest that my baby was the child of one of the soldiers and not of his cousin, the Minister. He knew full well that this was impossible. I didn't care; I was leaving his home, and that was my final decision.

That weekend, I packed up my luggage and made my way up to the teachers' compound at Empress Mine. I was assisted by an army sergeant major, a man I knew well from my time with the freedom fighters; he had been one of their bravest and most responsible members, and one of the few to mourn the death of my father; he had been away in Maputo at the time of his murder. When the sergeant first saw me at Empress Mine School, he cried in sympathy as I told him the story of my subsequent life. He took me to meet his beautiful wife, and promised to look after me like his own little sister. He definitely kept his promise; by the time the army truck had come to collect my bags, the sergeant had already made sure that my new house was well-furnished and organised for a local girl to take care of the baby while I was at work. When I wrote of the move to my mother, she insisted on sending one of my younger brothers to check that everything was alright; he arrived with one of our cousins, ! a girl who had offered to help me.

Things had definitely taken a turn for the better; I was now really enjoying the teaching and my house had filled up with family. The school education authority were showering me with praise, even as Mr R.B.K did his best to make sure they sacked me. When the headmaster tragically died, the deputy took over his position, creating a vacancy that I was selected to fill. All my effort and hard work had finally paid off, and I had soon become a household name throughout the region. I got on well with my colleagues, and, on Thursdays, I would join the Methodist Women's Fellowship in prayer and choir practice. Thanks to good old Miss Subinda, I could read sheet music half-decently, which was enough to assist as our group entered a district choir competition. I was the youngest member, but the other women treated me with considerable respect, and regularly invited me to their houses for lunch after church on a Sunday.

CHAPTER 15

The choir competition was run in Kadoma town and sponsored by a senior government official, the Minister for Local Government and Rural and Town Planning, who was both a committed member of the Methodist Church and the butt of endless jokes based on his legendary lack of beauty. It was said that, when visiting a newly-built dam, the Minister looked in the water, saw his reflection and commented on how quickly hippos had moved into the area! People can be so mean at times; little did they know that this Minister would one day boast to me about being the most handsome man in the Cabinet - the best-dressed, best-educated and best-spoken man in Zimbabwe, aside from the President, of course!

As Kadoma was his constituency, the Minister was often in our area; I saw him at a number of rallies, as well as when he was handing out trophies for the winners of the choir competition. Our Methodist Women's Fellowship claimed first prize, and, when I went to the stage to collect my award, the Minister gripped my hand firmly and secretly tickled the palm of my hand with his finger. At previous meetings, I had often caught him gazing at me from a distance, but this was the first time he'd confirmed his attraction. The thick-lipped, gap-toothed smile he gave me sent shivers down my spine; I never thought for one second that this man would write another chapter in my life.

One weekend, the army sergeant came to my house with his wife and the news that the whole Fifth Brigade had been ordered to leave Empress Mine. This I was saddened to hear, not simply because I'd be losing good friends, but also as the army had acted as an effective line of defence for the school; without the soldiers, our houses and building were bound to be targets for thieves. A disturbing rumour had also got into circulation that the village headman was seeking to take control of the teacher's compound and force us to pay him some rent; there was talk of him cutting the electricity and water supply until we agreed to cough up. Amid this uncertainty, some of the less local teachers moved on. I stayed, hoping to hold on until I'd saved enough money to enrol at the University of Zimbabwe. I definitely had no problems living in a place without taps and electricity; I had done so for most of my life and had the skills and experience to survive in more extreme conditions than these.

The army moved out quickly, leaving Empress Mine an isolated and spooky shell of itself. At night, darkness would engulf the whole place, and I often heard looters smashing their way into the empty buildings. Each pay-day, I would leave for Kadoma town or Kwe-Kwe to do some shopping and get a taste of town life. I'd always make sure to grab some fish and chips for dinner, and carry more home for my daughter and her babysitter. By this point, my brother had emigrated to Australia to train as a Methodist preacher. I was really missing my family, and longed for the next school holiday when I would finally be able to visit my mother and son. This time, I'd bring the boy back with me to Zhombe.

It was a Saturday afternoon. I was marking essays, enjoying the sunshine, sat out on the veranda. I heard the sound of a car approaching and wondered vaguely who it might be. As I looked up, the strangely familiar sight of a big black Mercedes came driving down the dust-blown road. Maybe the Minister of Education had realised his mistake and arrived to apologise. Maybe he had come for his baby. I stood up and waited for whoever was inside to emerge. Two men in black suits came out; one who I took as the driver, the other, who I knew well by sight, was the bodyguard of the Minister of Local Government.

I greeted them politely and asked the childminder to bring out some extra chairs. The two men introduced themselves as Eddie - the bodyguard - and Chamu - the driver. Eddie spoke with authority; as he unbuttoned the jacket of his suit, I noticed a gun tucked indiscreetly into his belt. I got the message: whatever they'd come for, I was supposed to comply. As it was, they'd come to pick me up and take me to Kadoma Ranch Motel, where the Minister was waiting to meet me. I asked for a few minutes to talk to my childminder and tell my next-door neighbour where I was going. Then I changed into a nice blue dress, with matching sandals and handbag. I made sure to take some money; I might be travelling in style, but who knew how I would end up returning.

We arrived at Kadoma Ranch Motel at half past three. On the way, I'd been thinking about things that my mother had said. She'd actually gone to school with the Minister for Local Government; he was older than her and had been very good at football, though he was remembered more for his ugliness than his skills on the pitch. At the motel, I was quickly ushered up to one of the rooms, with no questions asked at reception. Eddie knocked on the door and the Minister opened it with a smile on his face.

Eddie saluted and left as I nervously entered the room; hearing the Minister lock the door behind me did nothing to diminish my apprehension. He came over towards me, and we sat together on a huge sofa by the window. His after-shave mingled with the strong scent of his breath as he rested his chubby hands on my knees. He thanked me for coming to see him, which was ironic seeing as his entourage had practically kidnapped me. Then he started talking about my father; asking how much I knew of the reasons for his death, and why I wouldn't give up on my quest for uncomfortable answers. He asked me what it would take to make me forget about what happened to my father and move on with my life; I replied that it wasn't about me, that I simply wanted to give my mother the chance to properly mourn her dead husband. Then came the veiled threats; the Minister told me that the President was unhappy with the letters I'd written to him and accusations I'd made against the Government.

"If a person lifts up too many stones," said the Minister, "sooner or later, they're bound to be bitten by a snake or a scorpion."

That wasn't all he had to say. As an overwhelming sense of deja-vu enveloped the scene, the Minister told me he'd taken a fancy to me from the very first time that we'd met. Apparently, he'd hired people to check up on me, and had finally decided that I was the one, and that now was the right time to make me his wife! The President himself had even provided approval! Oh God, could this really be happening again?

Lie after lie after lie. He said he'd fallen in love with me so deeply that he was struggling to concentrate on his job. He said that his supposed wife - who was Cuban, and who he had met, unsurprisingly, at the Africa Centre in London - was not really his wife at all; they had lived together in England, and their first two children had died as a result of her neglect. She had turned into a violent alcoholic, and when the Minister returned to Zimbabwe, he had left her behind. It was only when she arrived on his doorstep, pregnant again and pleading for help, that he reluctantly, and oh so charitably, took her back. God, did these ministers synchronise their stories or what? This was pretty much exactly what the first one had told me! Apparently, this new minister's wife was very much a drunk, who often embarrassed him by pissing in public. As a Christian, he had taken her in, looked after her and found her a job. As a respectable man, what he wanted most of all was a dignified and beautiful wife - someone like me! He claimed to be fully aware of my ready-made family and only too happy to take us all in.

My "Mills and Boon" memories were fading fast. Here I was, in a shoddy motel, hearing some dodgy manifesto in place of the sweet words of love. Was this all I was worth? A public convenience that powerful dirty old men could use as they wished. Did I deserve this for being so stupid as to ever let it happen at all? I felt trapped; I was still very young - a mere child in need of protection. These respectable men in sharp designer suits were much older than even my parents, and none of them seemed capable of treating me well.

Once, I even slept with Mugabe himself. It happened after I'd been to his office to talk about my father's death. Like a vulture over a carcass, he seized his own chance to enjoy a piece of the meat. When I think of him now, it's difficult to remember anything over than his naked dark body, unadmirable and old, lounging on the massive bed at the state house. There was a pistol on that bed, and a calabash full of marijuana that the President smoked whenever we broke off from the act. Of course, I wasn't the only young girl to have slept in that bed. In a way, I should count myself lucky; many of the others seemed to simply disappear.

The Minister had moved closer and was now touching me all over my body. When I turned to look at him, I was met with the horrible sight of his huge lips coming straight in to suffocate me. Was I being raped, or were we making love? The lines grew blurry, as the Minister climbed on top and my chest began to burn. I could hear my blue dress tearing along its seams as he grunted like a pig. The whole room started to spin. God, this man was heavy! It was like being under the weight of a pregnant elephant; my crushed ribs were becoming unbearably hot. What made it worse was that I had nothing to hold on to; the Minister's body was flabby and soft, with no muscles to grip to. I was still trembling when he carried me to bed and covered me with blankets. It was the middle of summer, but to me it was freezing. My stomach was churning. The Minister went to the bathroom, relieved himself, and then walked out the motel door. As he turned the lock from outside, I burst into uncontrollable tears. It had happened again; I'd been naive and fallen into the trap. Who would believe what had happened? Who could I tell such a shameful thing? In everyone's eyes, it is always the fault of the woman.

It was seven o'clock when the door finally opened. The Minister stood in the doorway with his bodyguard and one of the hotel porters, pushing a shiny silver trolley full of food. Only the Minister entered the room; he came and sat beside me and opened the plastic bags he was holding. Inside were two dresses, two bras and two pairs of pants. There was also a silk night dress with a matching gown, a toothbrush, and a jar of Ingram's Camphor cream. I took this to mean he was sorry, and that he wished me to spend the whole weekend with him. I barely touched the meal. All I wanted to do was fall sleep and then never wake up. I barely heard the Minister as he insisted that, now we were officially a couple, he wanted me to live in Harare, and not out in the sticks on my own. How deeply caring! He said that I was to move by the end of the year at the latest, and that I should hand in my notice at Empress Mine as soon as I started on Monday. All of my things would be brought to the city; the Minister would personally arrange for it. As his words slowly sank in, I saw my life once more being transformed right in front of my eyes.

This time, there was simply no way that my mother could know; it would break her heart and quite possibly kill her. The next week end, I took a bus to her village and explained that I was transferring jobs because the place where I was had become very dangerous. She suggested that I should leave the baby with her for a while, at least until things were settled. I agreed; though it was incredibly sad, I knew that it would be better for her to be with my mother than with me in Harare, where I could hardly be sure of the future. My little boy had grown, and was already helping with the family chores: herding the cattle, or helping to water the vegetable garden. I went back to Empress Mine School and served out my notice. Every Friday, the big black Mercedes would turn up to take me away for "romantic" weekends at the Ranch Motel. Sometimes, the Minister would take me as far as Kariba, or Chimanimani, or Masvingo, or even Victoria Falls. I slowly grew comfortable with the lifestyle, but was far from in love; the man was so old and ugly, but too powerful for me to refuse. What else could I have done?

Perhaps I should have at least used contraceptives to avoid another unwanted pregnancy. There were plenty of Family Planning Clinics in Zimbabwe; I could easily have walked into one and picked up a few magic tablets. But young women who took the pill were often cruelly labelled, and, anyway, sex was such a random act for me that it was almost impossible to prepare for; my relationships were always irregular, and my sex life came and went without warning. Most of the time, sex simply didn't figure on the agenda; it was only when some big man took a fancy that I ever got involved. My own private fantasies proved no more than shadows, like the perfect gentlemen of those "Mills and Boon" novels.

CHAPTER 16

I said my farewells at Empress Mine School. I had grown to love the place, and felt very sad to be leaving. All my belongings had been packed in the back of a big truck from Swift Removals; as for me, the big black Mercedes Benz was waiting with its engines running, ready to head off down the road.

It was a pretty special goodbye; there were tears and hugs and kisses, and I got plenty of presents from my students, fellow teachers and friends from the village. On the Saturday, the Methodist Women's Fellowship visited to spend the whole day singing and praising the Lord, blessing me with all kinds of good wishes. They all brought presents, too; in return, I gave each of them some of my kitchen utensils, and some of them my clothes and precious items. I gave the church about two hundred dollars, and laid on a farewell feast of bread and jam and tea and rice. Everyone ate and some left with food to take back to their homes. I even baked up a whole load of my famous fat cooks, which brought tears to the eyes of all of the women; they reminded them of our first cooking lesson under the big fig tree, when I taught them how to make those delicious crispy round cookies!

The crowning moment was when the local headman came to say his personal goodbye. He presented me with an ox-hide mat, made from a bull he had slaughtered at one of his traditional ceremonies. I felt honoured and valued, if slightly reluctant to accept a gift which was based on something that went against my religious beliefs. I took it, anyway, and knew that I'd done the right thing - after all, it was only a dead bull's skin.

I arrived in Harare at three o'clock in the afternoon. The city was bustling with people, and the dramatic siren of the President's motorcade was soon following us down the road, forcing my driver to move to the side and give way. It was definitely an impressive convoy: an open army truck, full of soldiers holding machine guns, followed by policemen on big motorbikes, police cars with flashing blue lights, and then the President's bullet-proof black limousine flanked by two big Mercedes and more policemen on motorbikes. A few extra unmarked cars with flashing lights followed behind, alongside another open army truck, with more soldiers bearing extravagant weapons. I felt like I was watching Armageddon! The whole street came to a stand-still for almost ten minutes; everyone at the side of the road saluted the President as his motorcade zoomed imperiously past on its way to the State House, or Parliament, or wherever they were heading.

When this interlude was over, we carried on along Samora Michael Way to the St Tropez flats which were to be my new home. I already had the keys to my flat, which the Minister's bodyguard had handed to me even before we'd set off from Empress Mine. I was excited; the St Tropez apartments were beautifully built and had been reserved for white people during the colonial era. Now, they were mainly occupied by senior civil servants. There was a caretaker, who kept the place secure and immaculate at all times. When I opened the door to my new home, I was happy to see that there was already some furniture attractively arranged: a black leather sofa, a television, a nice radio, and a long coffee table with a zebra-hide rug spread out nicely below it. The bedroom had an en-suite bathroom and huge fitted wardrobes. The kitchen was well stocked with food. I even had an electric kettle!

I unpacked, then sat myself down on the sofa to think. I'd been handed this luxury life for free, but still wasn't sure why. I was surrounded by neighbours, but completely alone, with little idea what to do with myself, and no-one who knew where I was. I hadn't even told my own mother. Suddenly, there was a knock at the door and the handle started to move. My heart flew up my throat and I jumped up to switch on the light. It was the Minister, holding a briefcase and a bunch of newspapers. He seemed happy to see me, and asked me to make him some tea; ah, that was why I was here - to be the Minister's wife and attend to all of his needs. This was the start of something long-term, something that I resisted from telling my mother, even when I returned to her during every school holiday to visit my children and show them I loved them. I just couldn't bring myself to tell mother that I was now living with that man who had once been the ugliest boy at her school.

Those trips to the village were my happiest times; it was so good to spend time with my children, but I always returned to Harare with a deeper understanding of my own personal misery. The new lifestyle I lived had its comforts, but I rarely enjoyed them; I'd very quickly realised that I'd made a mistake, but now felt completely ensnared. The Minister would sometimes sleep at the flat; other times, he would come over for lunch, or to freshen up for an afternoon Parliament session. A lot of people around the apartments knew what was happening, and I felt their suspicions fall heavily upon me. Life became very stagnant, and I missed my job very much. Once, when I told the Minister that I still wanted to find my father's body, he menacingly warned me that people disappear very fast when they start to talk too much. He didn't want anything like that to happen to me.

It was in the month of July that I noticed I'd missed my last period. When I told the Minister, he suggested that, if I was actually pregnant, I should go to a good doctor up on the Avenues and get an abortion. There was no way I'd allow that to happen; if I was pregnant once more - which it turned out I was - then I was definitely keeping the baby. The Minister reluctantly agreed, and suggested I should move to Kwe-Kwe, where one of his younger brothers worked as a businessman, when the baby was born.

One day, when I was about five months into the pregnancy, I lay on the sofa at the St Tropez flat, taking my regular afternoon nap, when an unexpected knock at the door woke me up. When I opened it, two women stormed in, pushing me around and slapping me hard on the face. Dazed and shocked, I retreated to the sofa and sat trembling as they ransacked the house, clearing out all of the food, before overturning my bed and leaving with a warning that they'd soon be back to get me again. When they'd gone, I rushed to the care-taker's office and called the Minister to let him know what had happened. He told me not to worry, and not to report the incident either; it was simply cheap thieves from the townships and the police would cause more trouble than they were worth. He was wrong; that incident was the start of a terrible time for me at St Tropez.

Two weeks later, the Minister had come over for lunch and was just about to head back to his office when somebody knocked at the door. Expecting his driver, the Minister opened it to see a young boy of about fifteen, who immediately threw a bundle of powdery sticks on the floor by the Minister's feet. As he attempted to force shut the door, the Minister's bare foot was pierced by one of the sticks and he instantly cried out in pain. Within minutes, he couldn't move and his right foot had swollen up like a football. The boy, of course, was long gone, but the bodyguard and driver had finally arrived and helped their boss into his car. I followed, locking the door behind me; strangely, I actually stepped on the powder and sticks but in me they seemed to have no reaction.

The Minister told his driver to take us as fast as he could to Karoi. With the infected foot now shining like the skin of an unripe avocado, the bodyguard called a senior official to spread word that the Minister had sprained his ankle badly. Officially, we were on our way to see a well-trained doctor in the Avenues; in reality, we were on our way to see the Minister's witch-doctor way out in a cave in the mountains.

I had never seen a real witch-doctor in action before. The driver parked the car a discrete distance away from the cave; with the Minister hobbling, we made our way slowly towards its dark mouth. Both the driver and bodyguard seemed to know the place very well - they had obviously been here before. Of course, it was widely rumoured that most leading government figures had their own witchdoctor to assist their campaigns and to keep them in power. But rumours are one thing; reality is entirely another.

As soon as we entered the cave, everyone started clapping loudly as a way of announcing our arrival. I was the quietest, following hesitantly behind, my heart beating faster than ever. The music of mbira instruments and all sorts of African rhythms and softly-sung songs started emanating from deeper within; as we approached the players, I saw some strange creature dancing to the tune of their music - a huge python dressed in colourful beads and cloth. If it hadn't been for the bodyguard grabbing me and warning me not to do anything stupid, I would have been out of there that very second. My hair was literally standing on end as we passed underneath the giant snake; this, I later discovered was a test of courage that all prospective patients had to pass; it was alleged that if an evil person approached the python, they would be bitten or suffer a terrible disease that would kill them within twenty-four hours.

Somehow, all four of us got through safely, and found ourselves face to face with the witch-doctor herself - an old lady, dressed in beads and a big-feathered hat, who was already in a trance and whistling weirdly. There was an overwhelmingly strange smell in the cave. The witch-doctor took a swig of water from a calabash and spat it at the Minister, who fell to the floor as if paralysed. Then she took a wooden spoon and placed it on his swollen foot. I was beginning to question my sanity as the old lady knelt on the ground by the Minister and started to bite into his foot, her sharp teeth drawing blood.

The Minister shrieked, and had to be held in place by his driver and bodyguard. After two or three bites, the witch-doctor started smearing some mucky green paste on the Minister's foot. Then she sprinkled water from the calabash and started to speak like a man. I noticed that her necklace was made up of bones, and on her feet she wore beads and bronze ornaments; I tell you, she was a complete shoe-in for best fancy dress at a Halloween party! The man's voice she spoke with said that the poison the Minister had been infected by had not been intended for him, but for me; had I stepped on it first, both my baby and I would surely have died. Slightly more reassuringly, the witch-doctor went on to say that I was well-protected by very powerful forces; the Minister didn't need to worry about me. Amazingly, I found myself in agreement with this crazy old lady; there was a very powerful being that was watching over me from above; even a witch-doctor would tremble at the mention of his name.

The Minister interpreted this pronouncement in a very different way; he seemed to believe that this powerful person was my father. On our very first night together, at the Ranch Motel, I had had a strange dream about my mother's home; my brother and I were out in the garden and had started to squabble over a watering can; as I pulled it away, I threw my right fist in his face.

That was the dream; in reality, I had struck out at the face of the minister, who saw this as a sign. He woke me up, my fist still pressed against his jaw, and began to apologise in a detached way as though he were speaking directly with my ancestors. It was just as well he reacted this way; I dreaded to think what the bodyguard would have done if he'd heard that I'd beaten his boss!

When the witch-doctor had finished her work, the Minister produced a wad of money and placed it on a clay plate that was already covered in snuff. He thanked the old lady and we made our way out of her horrible home. On the way back to Harare, the Minister suggested I should get ready to leave the next day for his brother's home in Kwe-Kwe. Danny, the Minister's brother, was a successful businessman with three wives and three nice big houses to match. He took turns in each house, but stayed as often as he could at the home of his youngest wife, a very beautiful, fair-skinned lady, who seemed to worship the ground that he walked on. In fact, all of Danny's wives treated him like a king, and perhaps rightly so; he was a giant with genuine charm and I doubt there were many women who could have stopped themselves falling in love. Even his last wife's younger sister, who was even more beautiful, but still studying in the final year of her O Levels, seemed enraptured with Danny, and it was obvious that he was lining her up to be wife number four. He took her out for expensive lunches, provided a chauffeur to take her to school, and even inspected her bedroom each day to ensure that the housemaids had done a good job and fresh flowers had been placed by her bed. Naturally, a silent war had developed between this girl and her older sister, who was slowly coming to terms with the fact that Danny would have to be spread even thinner. Still, she clearly didn't want to loose her big beautiful house, so she resigned herself to the idea that it was better to share her own husband with her sister than another complete stranger; at least that way all the family would benefit.

Danny always reminded me of the Godfather; I used to jokingly refer to his family as the "Gambachinos". He was a very kind man, with a great sense of humour, but an inescapable air of menace that could send shivers down my spine. He was the sort of guy who could kill you while laughing. Anyway, the family welcomed me kindly; I was given my own private quarters in the youngest wife's house, which was built up on top of a hill. A driver would regularly take me to the local ante-natal clinic, where the nurses would attend to me as soon as I arrived. Even the Senior Midwife would always welcome me like a special envoy, ushering me into a room where the doctor would already be waiting. It made me feel quite guilty to be pulled to the front of the queue; I always kept my head down and avoided eye contact with the other women, many of whom were at least as far pregnant as me and had probably come a long way on public transport or even by foot. It was awful to hear some of them grumbling as I was pulled to the front of the queue.

At weekends, the Minister would always come over to visit. A special meal would be prepared and the best cutlery would be laid on the big ivory table. I was still deeply uncomfortable with the whole situation, especially the fact that my mother knew nothing. One night, when I was feeling particularly disturbed by this thought, I took out a pen and paper and began to write one of the longest letters I've ever written. I knew I had to apologise; I knew I had to come clean to my mother; she needed to know the truth, no matter how terrible it would look like to her. I could feel the baby kicking against my belly as I went on my knees and asked God to forgive me. I promised Him that I would change my life and reform. I swore that night that I would never sleep with the Minister again. Finally feeling at peace, I slept beautifully until the morning.

When the Minister arrived the following weekend, I lied to him that the hospital had advised me not to play around any more because the baby's head was lodged at a dangerous angle and my pelvis had become very tight. It was all made-up mumbo-jumbo, but it worked a treat; the Minister, of course, was disappointed, but who wants to be responsible for damaging their own baby? That night, his hands folded between his legs, he slept with his body facing away from mine. It was fantastic! The next weekend, he came but didn't sleep at the house; instead, he drove on to a "conference" in Bulawayo, which probably meant he was visiting another girlfriend.

On 11th February - the date sticks in my mind - I received a long letter of reply from my mother. She was not much surprised at my news; she had already guessed that something was up, and had been praying for me every day. She said she was missing me very much, that she still loved me, and that I was still her little girl. She included a prayer and a number of verses from the Bible. She told me to come home soon after the delivery, and said that I should never be ashamed of myself. I was amazingly touched to read her kind words; it was almost as if she were sat in the room right beside me. I could smell her sweat in my nostrils, and was overwhelmed by the strength of her love.

As I stood up to go and hide the letter away, warm water started to run down my legs. It was time; my new baby was ready to come. I felt a sharp pain, and my stomach tightened; I splashed slowly back to the bedroom to clean myself up, then changed into my maternity dress, picked up the baby bag that was already packed, and knocked at the door of Danny's wife's bedroom. In no time, an ambulance had arrived; Danny's wife travelled with me as her husband laughed down the phone to the Minister. I was in terrible pain, breathing in and out what felt like a thousand times a minute. No matter what anyone tells you, giving birth is the most painful experience in any woman's life!

The next thing I knew I was in the labour ward, and things were moving fast. I was walking up and down, swearing at any and every thing that I saw, like a tormented woman on the verge of a nervous breakdown. Hot and confused, I decided to take off my clothes. Unsurprisingly, the midwives grew quickly annoyed, though some clearly found the scene extremely amusing. Stark naked, I walked away from them, and soon found myself in the male ward; it drove me wild to see all those lucky men lying there who could never know how to sympathise with my pain. I shouted at them, forgetting that they too were sick in their own different ways, before the midwives caught me and hauled me away to the delivery room.

Tying me down on the bed, they told me that behaving in such a ridiculous way could threaten the life of my baby. That thought cleared my head; all I wanted to do now was push as hard as I could until the pain went away. I felt as though I could hear people shouting at me from a distance, then suddenly there was that first fateful cry from my baby and everyone was congratulating me - it was a perfect boy, already hungry for his very first feed!

I stayed for one night at the hospital. The next day, I was picked up and driven back to Danny's house, where I stayed for two weeks before being picked up again and dropped back at the apartment in Harare. I was determined to stay at St Tropez for six weeks before leaving for my mother's home with the baby. I no longer wanted to continue my relationship with the Minister; it was wrong, and by now I had realised that he had little intention of marriage. Luckily, the Minister didn't wish to sleep with me; he realised I was still tender from the birth and tradition demanded he wait for six weeks. Perfect!

The flat, when I returned, was immaculately clean, and everything I needed for the baby had been bought. There were fresh flowers on the coffee table, and cards of congratulations from the Minister, his driver and bodyguard, a few of my neighbours and even one from the President himself! That first afternoon, the Minister came over and held his baby for a long while. Part of me wanted to tell him there and then that I was planning to leave, but, in the end, I simply couldn't spoil this special union between father and son. Also, if I told him nearer the time, it would give him less time to interfere with my plans.

Then, one day, my baby disappeared. I was outside in the garden, hanging his nappies and clothes on the line; it had become my routine to do this each morning after bathing and feeding the baby, who I left in the flat, swathed in blankets and lying content on the sofa. Hanging up the clothes was only a half-hour's job at the most, and I would regularly pop back inside for a check. This time, I had been outside for less than ten minutes when I noticed the door was open much wider than I'd left it. Perhaps, it had been blown by the wind, but I decided to have a look inside for reassurance. It was not forthcoming; as I walked towards the sofa, I saw to my horror that the baby had gone.

I rushed into the bedroom: nothing. I called out in a panic, as if he could ever have answered. Then I ran to the caretaker's flat and used his phone to call direct to the Minister. The number was engaged; when I rang up his secretary, she said that the Minister was busy on the other line. I couldn't waste any more time; I needed the police to put the whole of Harare at a stand-still - if not the whole of the country! My baby had been stolen! Maybe by those terrible people who were known to steal babies and sell them to businessmen, who were convinced that the innocence of a baby - even a dead baby, kept close by to their shop - would encourage their customers to spend money like children.

I set off running towards Mukwati buildings, constantly looking around for a sign or a clue. When I reached the Minister's building, his driver and bodyguard seemed surprised to see me. I didn't wait to speak to his secretary, barging straight into his office, where the Minister was sat at his desk with a look of worry already on his face. Something told me he knew that our baby was missing, and that he probably knew where he was. Trembling and shouting, I demanded to know what had happened. The Minister simply told me to keep calm, to leave it all to him and definitely not to go to the police or the papers. It was his wife, he was convinced, who had stolen our baby; she was also the one behind all of the terrible incidents that had happened in St Tropez. She knew about our affair, and now she was after my blood.

The Minister asked his driver and bodyguard to drop me back at the flat; he promised he would come over that evening to talk. Reluctantly, I got in the Mercedes, unable to say for sure if I believed him or not. As we entered the gates at St Tropez, the driver gave way to a blue and white taxi; seconds later, as we reached the drive of my flat, I saw the caretaker standing outside the front door with my baby. The car was still slowing as I dived out and snatched back my child. The caretaker, bemused by the whole situation, simply said that the taxi had been sent to drop off the baby; there had been nobody else in the car but the driver. I held my baby so tightly and started to sob as the driver and bodyguard walked me back to my flat and opened the door. They checked the whole house before leaving and insisted that I lock the door behind them. I was left vulnerable and scared, with a terrible awareness that I was no longer safe in my very own flat.

True to his word, the Minister came round later that evening. His face looked a little puffed up; he had apparently had a fight with his wife, who had punched him. It was not the first time this had happened; sometimes, when she was drunk, his wife would even use a belt on him to humiliate him in public. I told the Minister of my plans: that I wanted to go back to my mother's home and find a new life for myself. I told him that I knew all he had promised was a lie, and that I was sick of being used by him and his colleagues.

The Minister begged me to stay, saying he would provide security and anything else that I wanted, but I stood my ground and refused all his offers. In the end, he reluctantly agreed I should go, asking only that I stay for a week in order to give him time to get some money together; he didn't want me to leave empty handed. He also insisted I should contact him without hesitation whenever I needed assistance. Softened by his apparent generosity, I agreed to stay for one final week. I would then go to visit my sister in Chiredzi and look for a house to rent - somewhere big enough for all of my children and I. Someone had told me that there were plenty of vacancies for temporary teachers in that area, so I knew that I stood a very good chance of finding a job.

Once more, things didn't work out to plan. Before that last week in Harare was over, I'd been forced to endure another terrible incident, one which threatened both my life and that of my baby. It was an event so far-reaching in its consequences that it changed the whole course of my life, leading me to end up in a strange land, far away from my family and everything I'd ever known; a land where snow falls in winter and the rich and the famous are found; a land of princes and princesses, where the streets are apparently paved with gold, where roads and railways reach under the ground, and where everyone's always so busy that time just never seems to stop. Some called this place a land of milk and honey, a land where dreams come true! For me, it was simply the next step in my miserable life; and the worst was still to come.

I will never forget the day that it happened, that this new chapter in my life unexpectedly began. It was the Friday following my baby's abduction, about seven o'clock in the evening. The Minister came to my flat as per usual; he told me he was on his way to a funeral in Mutare - one of the regional governors had sadly passed away. He brought out a huge envelope filled with almost two thousand dollars and gave it to me with the advice that I should leave immediately for my mother's home. I couldn't understand why he wanted me to get going so quickly; it was already evening and I didn't want to go out with my baby at night. Plus, if he was going to Mutare, who would be here to help me with my luggage. Yet the Minister seemed deeply disturbed, and insisted that I leave with the baby on the night train to Gweru. he left in a hurry, not even saying goodbye; as he left I got the distinct impression that he was being followed.

I went straight to the caretaker's flat; perhaps he would help me to pack up my things. I was planning to leave most of my stuff, coming back at some later date to collect it, but the caretaker claimed it was too late to start packing and rushing for the night train, especially with such a young baby. He advised me to wait for the morning, when he would come to the flat with his wife and make sure that everything went well. So I stayed, and we ate, and when the baby was sleeping, he walked me back to my flat. The place was very well lit, and, at first, I didn't think much when I noticed the front door had been left on the latch; maybe the Minister had returned in my absence. I put my son down on the sofa and went into the kitchen to make up his milk. The kettle was already warm.

We went into the bedroom together. The doors of my huge fitted wardrobes stood half-open; they were mirrored and I couldn't remember having left them ajar. As I put my baby to bed in his cot, I suddenly started hearing voices from inside the wardrobe. Then from the bathroom. Five women emerged; two of them holding guns.

"You've had enough warnings," they screamed, "this time we've come here to kill you!". I tried to plead with them, but they simply laughed in my face. They held me down, stripped me naked and tied me to the bed. They took newspapers from a pile in the corner of the room, stuffed some in my mouth and put others right under the bed. Then they set light to the bedroom curtains and different parts of the flat, and waited for the blaze to get going. Black smoke was quickly infecting the air, and I started to cough and choke as I reached for the keys that those witches had thrown on the bed, just slightly out of the grasp of my fingers. My poor baby was starting to suffocate, too; I felt hopeless and knew we would suffer a terrible death. Why couldn't they have just taken the baby and left me to die? Instead, all they'd taken were my best clothes and all of the Minister's, as well as the two thousand dollars, which I'd left on a shelf in the wardrobe. Absorbing the cries and breathless gasp of my baby, my panicking mind hurriedly faded to black.

The next day, I woke at Parireyatwa Hospital. Neighbours had apparently seen smoke coming out of the ventilation system and the fire brigade had been called. We were barely alive when they found us. Unsurprisingly, the media had caught wind of the story, and my baby and I were secretly transferred to a private hospital to escape their prying eyes. It still spread on the radio; my mother was told the terrible news by the head teacher of my former primary school.

The Police Commissioner came to interview me in hospital. Right from the start, he tried to persuade me to change my statement and claim that burglars had caused the fire, not the Minister's wife and her friends. I told him I was not prepared to tell lies; that I knew the perpetrator, and had met her several times; and that, expecting me to die, she had made no attempt to disguise her appearance on the night of the attack. I couldn't understand why he would want me to change from this statement.

The next thing I knew, I was being transferred once again, this time to a special hideaway, where my baby and I were provided with an armed police guard. We kept on moving; first to a police training depot, then to the Oasis Hotel, even, on one occasion, to a deserted training camp outside of the city. The Minister or his drivers would bring doctors to examine us, and, sometimes, we would be taken to a specialist foreign doctor, who seemed very angry at the way I was treated. My baby and I were being kept like prisoners; when my mother came to find us, no-one could say where we were. She was inconsolable, and cried all the way back to her village.

Repeatedly, I was questioned by both plain clothes and uniformed officers. Every time, they would tell me to change my story; even the Commissioner of the Criminal Investigation Department was brought in to persuade me. Over and over again, they would ask how much it would cost to get me to drop all the charges and forget the whole thing. Only two junior investigating officers ever tried to get justice done; for that, they were paid in threats and pressure, and obstructed from doing their job.

One day, while I was in hiding at the police training depot, the Minister came to see me with his driver and bodyguard. He entered the house alone and sat down beside me. Instinctively, I moved away; I didn't want him to smell my wounds, which sometimes blistered and stank. Still now, I couldn't cover my body fully; whatever I wore would stick to the open wounds. When I was inside, I wrapped myself up in a bed sheet, which was what I was wearing that day when the Minister came to assault me. He moved close, pushed me down on the sofa, and then raped me. The pain from my wounds was excruciating.

Afterwards, I was deeply ashamed. I felt bruised and violated, sore and frightened. I wanted to die and promised myself that as soon as night arrived, I would escape into the forest and hang myself from the tallest tree. No one would find me and I would never be buried; I didn't deserve that respect. Then I thought of my son; leaving him in the hands of these brutal beasts was something I just couldn't do. Somehow, I had to hold on, despite all my pain and despair. My unhealed wounds were now bleeding; most of the burns were on my thighs so sex was the cruellest act of all. My baby had a big open wound on his leg; despite his innocence, it was clear that the trauma had invaded him, too.

A month later, when the doctor came to see me, we were both shocked to find out I was pregnant. When I told him that the Minister had raped me, he simply nodded his head, though I could see that his eyes were swelling with tears. When the doctor left that day, he gave me some pills and told me to take them if I ever felt that I couldn't go on. He said he would not come back to treat me under these conditions; if they tried to force him, he would go to the papers and make his escape off to England, where most of his family were currently living. I took those tablets and flushed them down the toilet. Being pregnant again reminded me of all of my children; how could I leave them alone; what would they think if I took my own life? The thought of my children was reinvigorating; my desire to live was now stronger than ever.

In the end, the Minister's wife was arrested and indicted for attempted murder and arson. She was detained for one night in police cells, then transferred to a posh hotel called the Jameson after instructions from the President himself. The Minister told me on one of his visits that the President had also instructed that I should be sent overseas to get decent treatment and enjoy a good rest. It was becoming increasingly difficult for me to get proper care in Zimbabwe, especially with the media now after the Minister like sharks.

The President didn't want one of his best men to have to be sacked; all in all, the easiest thing was to get me right out of the country. Photographers came to take my passport pictures, which the Minister took to the Attorney General's office. A passport was soon obtained under my name, with my baby's attached. We were to immediately leave Zimbabwe for the United Kingdom; I wasn't even given the chance to say farewell to my children and mother, who was still desperately searching for me, nearly six whole months after the fire had happened.

I was told that the Zimbabwean High Commissioner would meet me at the airport in London. This arrangement had apparently been made by the President himself. It wouldn't be the first time that I'd been on a plane. Once, flying to Victoria Falls with the Minister, I'd helped to escort the Prime Minister of Australia to our nation's greatest sight. I had been given the privilege of guarding the sword of Zimbabwe - an honour very few have ever known. The sword was made of gold and silver and diamonds; it was very beautiful and heavy, but I managed it well. It felt like I was carrying my whole country in my hands; this time, the role had been reversed, and my country was preparing to drop me.

All of my clothes had been stolen or burnt in the fire. Before the flight, the Minister brought a few items for me and the baby to take on our journey. There was a pair of orange tennis shoes, a black dress with an open red cardigan, two nappies and a sling for the baby, together with a towel and a small bag that would have to make do as our suitcase. That was all he brought; he insisted the High Commissioner would have everything else that I needed ready and waiting in England. I would have a house, and everything would be arranged; I was to stay for a year, enjoy expert treatment, then return home to a reconstructed life in Zimbabwe.

When I arrived at Gatwick, the first thing that hit me was the cold. I was shivering, and everyone around me was wearing heavy dark coats, some with added scarves and gloves. My wounds were hurting me badly. I looked very different from everyone else and everything was exceptionally strange. I couldn't understand anything that was said, though I knew for sure it was English. I was in a strange land, very far away from home, and soon realised, to my horror, that there was no-one at the airport to meet me. The High Commissioner, as it turned out, was not even in London; he had travelled to Dublin and wasn't aware of my existence at all. My only hope was an "uncle" - one of my mother's distant cousins, who I knew lived in London.

While the authorities attempted to find him, I was kept in a detention zone. I was in a terrible state, my wounds were stinking, and the baby had soiled his nappy so badly that it was dripping out and running down the back of my dress. My tennis shoes were no match for the cold concrete on which I now walked. I was hungry and dizzy and confused; all I could do was tell the immigration officers the truth and hope for the best. What other choice did I have?

My uncle eventually came. He took us to his girlfriend's house; she didn't want to have us.

Once, I'd believed that God lived in England. I used to think that all of our spirits passed through this country on their way up to heaven. Or possibly that England was heaven itself. Now I knew different. Here I was, in the greatest nation of all, abandoned, homeless, alone and unnoticed. I had been sent here to die like an animal, and not one single person gave a damn who I was.

I felt like pure junk; an unknown foreigner who never existed. If I had died at that time, no-one would ever have traced me. If I had died at that time, I would have simply vanished from the face of the earth. Just like my father before me.

Other publications on sale:

Out of Zimbabwe by Debra Mina Chidakwa
ISBN:
Price:
In the second part of her autobiography, Debra Chidakwa recounts her struggle for survival as a homeless refugee in the UK, from almost freezing to death in a cemetery to encountering her former lover, the Zimbabwean Minister for Education, in his new role as Deputy Manager of the World Bank! Along the way, she battles illness, betrayal, the death of her son and the dangers of falling in love, to once more reveal the resilience of the human heart.

Songs from the heart by Debra Mina Chidakwa
ISBN: 18454990150
Price: £7.99
"I wrote these poems during times when I had little hope left. With my children especially, I wanted to share all my pain and my love. I wanted to empower them and enable them to recognise their value on earth. The time had come for me to speak out and empty my heart in these poems. I hope you enjoy them."
Debra Mina Chidakwa

Printed in the United Kingdom by
Lightning Source UK Ltd., Milton Keynes
142265UK00001B/67/P

9 781845 492878